RELIGION, ECONOMICS, AND PUBLIC POLICY

IRONIES, TRAGEDIES, AND ABSURDITIES OF THE CONTEMPORARY CULTURE WARS

ANDREW D. WALSH

PRAEGER

Westport, Connecticut
London

Library of Congress Cataloging-in-Publication Data

Walsh, Andrew D., 1965–
    Religion, economics, and public policy : ironies, tragedies, and absurdities of the
contemporary culture wars / Andrew D. Walsh.
        p. cm.
    Includes bibliographical references and index.
    ISBN 0-275-96611-9 (alk. paper)
        1. Economics—Religious aspects—Christianity—History—20th century. 2. United
States—Economic policy. I. Title.

BR115.E3 W33 2000
261.8'5—dc21   99-088505

British Library Cataloguing in Publication Data is available.

Library of Congress Catalog Card Number: 99-088505
ISBN: 0-275-96611-9

First published in 2000

Praeger Publishers, 88 Post Road West, Westport, CT 06881
An imprint of Greenwood Publishing Group, Inc.
www.praeger.com

Printed in the United States of America

Copyright Acknowledgment
Excerpts from *Pastoral Letters of the United States Catholic Bishops: Volume I,
1792–1940.* Copyright © 1984 United States Catholic Conference, Inc.,
Washington, DC. Used with permission. All rights reserved.

43095872

Contents

Preface

My passion for exploring the relationship between religion, economics, and public policy began when I was a child in Chicago's Sunset Hotel, and it was deepened by my experiences in rural Illinois. Even as a child, I could sense that people's views on religion played some role in their attitudes toward wealth and poverty. Since then, I have had the opportunity to read many of the classic statements by theologians, social scientists, and historians. As a scholar of religion, my goal is to present insights into all of the religions while claiming to represent none of them—an impossible goal capable of various degrees of approximation.

When acknowledging those people who have contributed to the completion of this book, I must first mention my students at Indiana University, Purdue University at Indianapolis (IUPUI), who have taught me very much. I would particularly like to acknowledge those students who have taken my courses in Religion and Contemporary American Politics; Religions, Ethics, and U.S. Society; and Comparative Religious Ethics.

I would also like to acknowledge the faculty members in the Religious Studies Department at IUPUI who have provided critical feedback through departmental colloquiums to very rough drafts of Chapters 1 and 4. In addition, I would like to thank some of my other colleagues at IUPUI for providing critical feedback to one or more chapters of this book: Luise Morton, John Tilley, Michael Burke, Steve Russell, and David Bivin. Dan Thompson provided critical feedback for the entire manuscript, and for his diligence I am particularly thankful. I would also like to thank Gary Dorrien and those participants in the Ethics Section of the Midwest region of the American Academy of Religion who responded to preliminary presentations of these materials. Finally, I would like to express my gratitude to Neal Riemer, an outstanding advisor, a great scholar, and a wonderful human being, without whose encouragement this book would not even exist. Obviously, none of these people are responsible for any of my errors in judgment, but their feedback made this a better book than it would have otherwise been. Outside of the academic world, my friends and family members who have made this book possible are too numerous to mention by name, but you know who you are, and I thank you.

Introduction

This book builds upon analysis of the "culture wars" as described by James Davison Hunter and refined by other scholars such as Richard John Neuhaus and George Weigel. In its most popular form, the culture wars thesis describes a nearly cosmic battle between (1) an "ecumenism of orthodoxy" that cuts across religious cleavages and (2) nominal religionists whose values have been shaped by secular elites in education, the media, and even liberal churches. The ecumenism of orthodoxy consists of *conservative* Evangelicals, Catholics, Mainline Protestants, and Jews who "order themselves, live by, and build upon the substance of a shared commitment to transcendent truths and the moral traditions that uphold them," while secular Americans and "nominal religionists" do not.[1] With respect to political economy, the orthodox are said to lean toward *laissez faire* capitalism while those who have drifted away from traditional religion lean toward liberal or Marxist views on political economy.[2]

In one respect, I have found this conceptualization of the American religious landscape to be very useful. Analyzing the arguments of religious leaders who have reduced politics into war by other means, I find numerous illustrations of five fallacies of wartime logic. First, cultural warriors, who refuse to allow empirical evidence stand in the way of ideology, assume that if Left is good, further to the left is better, or if Right is good, further to the right is better. Second, the combatants present false dichotomies: either you are for us or you are against us. Between "us" and "them," they see no alternatives. Third, culture wars foster the conclusion that "the enemy of my enemy must be my friend." Fourth, cultural warriors believe that humiliating the enemy is a necessary prerequisite for a lasting peace; thus, they insist that there be no negotiations, no compromises and no face-saving maneuvers. Fifth, cultural warriors conclude that if our side cannot win the war, we must poison the wells so that nobody wins. In the process of divorcing ends from means, they often become what they hate. These five fallacies provide deeper insights into key ironies, tragedies, and absurdities of religion and American politics.

While some elements of the culture wars thesis shed light on religion and politics in contemporary America, other elements are problematic. Most significantly for this book, I challenge the assumption by Hunter, Neuhaus, Weigel and others that orthodox religionists identify with *laissez faire* capitalism while those who have drifted away from traditional religion embrace liberal or Marxist views on political economy. Inasmuch as my own writing has a polemical intent, it is to challenge the assumption of those on the Left or Right who insist that "orthodox" views on religion lead to *laissez faire* views on political economy while secularization leads to liberal or Marxist views on political economy.

This book will be divided into two parts. The first part explores the historical relationships between religious communities and political economy. More specifically, it analyzes the role of religious communities in creating, legitimating, and dismantling America's welfare state. Chapter 1 clarifies the shifting position of evangelicals and fundamentalists toward Social Darwinism and provides background for the position of the New Christian Right on health care reform and welfare reform. Chapter 2 highlights the "Mainline" Protestant leadership's shift from a sensible realistic position to a sectarian stance with a marginal influence on public policy debates. Chapter 3 illuminates the potential for the Catholic Church to rise above the culture wars in order to shape America's new vital center on economics and public policy, while foreshadowing how the Left or the Right (depending upon whether the issue is welfare reform or health care reform) can drag the Catholic Church into the culture wars by relating an economic policy to the issue of abortion. Chapter 4 refutes simplistic views that secularization corresponds with liberal or socialist agendas and religion corresponds with *laissez faire* capitalism.

The second part of this book describes the role of religious communities in the public policy debates surrounding health care reform (the defeat of the Health Security Act that sought to provide a federal guarantee of universal access to health care for all Americans) and welfare reform (the passage of the Personal Responsibility and Work Opportunity Reconciliation Act that eliminated the federal guarantee of a safety net for poor Americans with children).

NOTES

1. James Davison Hunter, *Culture Wars: The Struggle to Define America* (New York: Basic Books, 1991), 126, 329 (footnote 16).

2. Ibid. Hunter is among those who assume that secularists have "deep humanistic concerns about the welfare of community," though he offers no empirical evidence to support this claim (45, 75–76). When talking about H. L. Mencken and William Jennings Bryan, he ignores the fact that Mencken was a fiscally conservative atheist and Bryan was a fiscally liberal fundamentalist (141–42). Although he is obviously familiar with William Jennings Bryan, he does not hesitate to identify orthodox Christianity with *laissez faire* capitalism (111–12, 128). [Orthodoxy literally means "right belief," and it is etymologically related to the word for doctrine.

Part I

Ironies of the Twentieth Century

From the Economic Liberalism of William Jennings Bryan to Social Darwinism in the New Christian Right

At the dawn of the twentieth century, a coalition of evangelical Christians led by William Jennings Bryan opposed the dissemination of Charles Darwin's theories. When William Jennings Bryan was embarrassed at the Scopes Monkey Trial of 1925, theologically conservative Christians were mocked as backward country bumpkins who resisted progress. According to Robert Liebman and Robert Wuthnow, this embarrassment, along with the failure of Prohibition, led most Evangelicals to withdraw from politics in the United States and to proclaim a sectarian witness:

For more than 50 years evangelicals kept studiously aloof from American politics. They sang hymns and tended to souls, but left the burdens of legislation and social policy to their more worldly counterparts in the Protestant mainstream. From time to time an occasional voice broke the self-imposed silence. . . . But these were the exceptions and even fellow fundamentalists tended to regard them with suspicion. . . . They were, by all indications, a declining remnant, destined to survive only by withdrawing from active confrontation with the secular age. . . . That their own pastors would lead a political movement seemed out of the question.[1]

Nevertheless, after five decades of avoiding political confrontation, the Moral Majority, the Christian Coalition, the Institute for Christian Economics, the Christian Freedom Foundation, Concerned Women for America, and Focus on the Family, among others, have initiated a new wave of political activism among Evangelicals. Ironically, many of these evangelical Christian movements have adopted a form of Social Darwinism to justify their critiques of welfare, health care reforms, affirmative action, and, in some cases, even philanthropy.

The transformation of the Christian Right is admittedly quite complex, and generalizations will be nuanced in light of the diversity of evangelical views on political economy. A more accurate historical reconstruction of Bryan's argument can shed light not only upon the past but also upon the present. The Left's historical reconstruction of William Jennings Bryan as a bumbling idiot has harmed both the Left and the Right. In humiliating Bryan, the Left failed to acknowledge his genuine insights. In embracing the academic Left's caricature of William Jennings Bryan, the New Christian Right has inverted Bryan's populist movement. In evangelical circles, William Jennings Bryan is remembered as a Christian martyr, the spokesperson for fundamentalist Christianity in the Scopes Monkey Trial, who was humiliated by the press and scorned by a secular society. With this image in mind, the New Christian Right fails to recognize that Bryan's political economy serves as one of the most powerful critiques of any attempt to reconcile *laissez faire*[2] capitalism with Christianity.

Three times, Bryan ran for president of the United States. Each time, he won the primary election only to lose the presidential election. He was an avid Democrat. He proposed a federal income tax, challenged the imperial relationship between the United States and the Philippines, supported women's suffrage, demanded that a labor representative serve in the president's cabinet, warned against returning the railroads to private ownership, and rejected a gold standard that would have prevented common laborers from borrowing money to buy their own homes.[3] In writing his biography, Donald Springen goes as far as to suggest, *"Bryan was, in fact, the father of the modern Democratic Party that Franklin D. Roosevelt later led with such greatness."*[4]

Bryan was concerned about the poor. Bryan was at least as wary of the concentration of power in big business as contemporary Evangelicals are of the dangers of big government. His economic proposals challenged the *laissez faire* assumptions of his Republican opponents. For example, Paolo Coletta explains Bryan's position on cutting taxes for the rich:

By reducing the tax rates on the highest incomes, and in other ways, "Big Business" was seeking to shift the burden of taxation from the profiteers and large corporations to the small corporations and to the masses. . . . He [Bryan] rejected the Republican philosophy that reducing taxes on the rich would release funds for investment in business, thus restoring prosperity, saying that if this was the intention of the bill then a provision should compel those who gained to actually invest in business and prohibit investment in tax-free bonds.[5]

Bryan was critical of a *laissez faire* theory of the state, critical of what later would be called *supply-side* or *trickle-down economics,* and critical of policies that favor the rich at the expense of the poor. Claims by philanthropists that private charities could compensate for any deficiencies in the market did not seem empirically justifiable. For William Jennings Bryan, these callous economic policies could not be reconciled with Christian compassion for the poor.

It is in the context of his political economy that liberals might empathize with Bryan's critique of Darwinism. It is unfortunate that Bryan's testimony at the Scopes Monkey Trial did not move beyond a defense of the literal truth of the Bible to articulate his fears about how the theory of evolution might serve as a normative framework for justifying the "selection" of responsible individuals through the "natural" processes of the free market. In an earlier argument, Bryan had stated:

The Darwinian theory represents man as reaching his present perfection by the operation of the law of hate—the merciless law by which the strong crowd out and kill off the weak. If this is the law of our development then . . . we shall turn backward toward the beast in proportion as we substitute it for the law of love.[6]

Bryan anticipated that evolution would not simply be a theory for describing the past. He feared that natural selection would serve as a normative model for constructing social theories that would undermine compassion for the poor.

Had William Jennings Bryan been able to present his speech, written to serve as the closing argument for the state in the *State of Tennessee v. John Thomas Scopes* (1925), historians might have a better understanding of the connection between Bryan's theological conservatism and his economic liberalism. Here Bryan reiterates his critique that the principle of "survival of the fittest" would be used to justify the cruelest social policies. He claims that "Nietzsche carried Darwinism to its logical conclusion."[7] He cites *Thus Spake Zarathustra*, in which Friedrich Nietzsche proclaims, "*I teach you the Superman*. Man is something that is to be surpassed. . . . What is the ape to man? A laughing-stock, a thing of shame. And just the same shall man be to the Superman: a laughing-stock, a thing of shame."[8] From Bryan's perspective, such notions undermined the fundamental dignity and equality of all human beings and could easily be used to justify the suffering and death of society's most vulnerable members in the name of social progress. Therefore, Bryan describes Nietzsche's notion of the "Superman" as a "damnable philosophy, and yet it is the flower that blooms on the stalk of evolution."[9]

The idea that the Superman need not treat inferior human beings with dignity and respect, in Bryan's view, completely undermines traditional morality. To draw attention to this point, Bryan quotes Nietzsche's text:

Become hard. To be obsessed by moral consideration presupposes a very low grade of intellect. We should substitute for morality the will to our own end, and consequently to the means to accomplish that. A great man, *a man whom nature has built up and invented in a grand style,* is colder, harder, less cautious, and more free from the fear of public opinion. He does not possess the virtues which are compatible with respectability, with being respected, nor any of those things which are counted among the virtues of the herd [emphasis added].[10]

The idea that the self-proclaimed Superman can simply dispense with traditional morality is incompatible with Bryan's view of Christianity.

Bryan also refers to Nietzsche's polemic, "The Antichrist," which dismisses Christianity as a sentimental tradition that "makes the strong and efficient man its typical outcast," takes "the part of the weak and the low," and "preserves what is ripe for extinction."[11] At this point, it is worth noting that *Nietzsche rejects religion for the opposite reason as Karl Marx.* Whereas Karl Marx assumes that the rich had created religion to drug the poor into passively accepting injustice in this lifetime in return for an eternal reward (heaven) or a better life next time (reincarnation), Friedrich Nietzsche assumes that the weak had created religion in order to fool the strong into feeling pity, guilt, and an obligation to provide them with charity. Interestingly, it is not the correlation between Christianity and the weak that Bryan rejects. Bryan accepts Nietzsche's assumption that the Christian faith encourages people to identify with the poor and the weak, but he opposes Nietzsche's conclusion that compassion is misguided because some human beings are ripe for extinction.

William Jennings Bryan typically identified Darwinism with Nietzsche, rather than Herbert Spencer and William Graham Sumner, the names most commonly associated with Social Darwinism. Perhaps Bryan perceived that Nietzsche's arguments were the most powerful, the most popular, and the most easily ridiculed at a time when many Americans were associating Nietzsche with German imperialism.[12] Like Nietzsche, however, Spencer and Sumner espoused a hard-nosed realism that has no pity for the suffering of the weak. Herbert Spencer explains:

Blind to the fact that under the natural order of things society is constantly excreting its unhealthy, imbecile, slow, vacillating faithless members, these unthinking, though well-meaning, men advocate an interference which not only stops the purifying process, but even increases the vitiation—absolutely encourages the multiplication of the reckless and incompetent by offering them an unfailing provision, and discourages the multiplication of the competent and provident by heightening the difficulty of maintaining a family.[13]

For William Jennings Bryan, the policy implications of Social Darwinism stood in sharp contrast to Jesus' "Sermon on the Mount," which pronounces blessings upon the merciful, the peacemakers, and the poor.

According to Bryan, Jesus' teachings (such as the narrative about the laborers in the vineyard who were all paid for a full day's work even though some were only able to work a short time) challenged the callousness of men like William Graham Sumner who counseled:

But the weak who constantly arouse the pity of humanitarians and philanthropists are the shiftless, the imprudent, the negligent, the impractical, and the inefficient, or they are the idle, the intemperate, the extravagant, and the vicious. Now the troubles of these persons are constantly forced upon public attention, as if they and their interests deserved especial consideration, and a great portion of all organized and unorganized effort for the common welfare consists in attempts to relieve these classes of people. . . . Now who is the Forgotten Man? He is the simple, honest laborer, ready to earn his living by productive work.[14]

While Sumner crusaded to make sure that hardworking American citizens were not forgotten, Bryan crusaded to make sure that the "hard teachings" of Jesus were not forgotten.

In his undelivered speech written for the state of Tennessee, William Jennings Bryan presents a quotation from another follower of Darwin. He does not identify the author but identifies the book as *The New Decalogue of Science,* from which he quotes:

Evolution is a bloody business, but civilization tries to make it a pink tea. Barbarism is the only process by which man has ever organically progressed, and civilization is the only process by which he has ever organically declined. . . . When you take man out of the bloody, brutal, but beneficent, hand of natural selection you place him at once in the soft, perfumed, daintily gloved, but far more dangerous, hand of artificial selection. And, unless you call science to your aid and make this artificial selection as efficient as the rude methods of nature, you bungle the whole task.[15]

As a politician, Bryan concludes that Darwin's theories of "natural selection" and "survival of the fittest" will be applied to public policies that justify the suffering and death of human beings in the name of progress.

Sometimes Darwin does describe evolution as a normative framework for social analysis and not merely as a biological theory. By all accounts, Darwin's theory was inspired by the social analysis of Thomas Robert Malthus in his *Essay on the Principle of Population.* Moreover, Darwin defers to Herbert Spencer, the most prolific of the Social Darwinists, in his use of language: "The expression often used by Mr. Herbert Spencer of the Survival of the Fittest is more accurate [than natural selection]."[16] Recognizing that Darwin clearly uses the theory of "survival of the fittest" to draw normative implications for *social policies,* William Jennings Bryan insightfully draws upon two quotations from Darwin's *The Descent of Man* in his undelivered speech for the state of Tennessee:

With savages the weak in body or mind are soon eliminated. . . . We civilized men, on the other hand, do our utmost to check the process of elimination; we build asylums for the imbecile, the maimed, and the sick; we institute poor laws; and our medical men exert their utmost skill to save the life of everyone to the last moment. There is reason to believe that vaccination has preserved thousands who from a weak constitution would formerly have succumbed to smallpox. Thus the weak members of civilized society propagate their kind. No one who has attended to the breeding of domestic animals will doubt that this must be highly injurious to the race of man.

The aid which we feel impelled to give to the helpless is mainly an incidental result of the instinct of sympathy, which was originally acquired as part of the social instincts, but subsequently rendered . . . more tender and widely diffused. . . . We must therefore bear the undoubtedly bad effects of the weak surviving and propagating their kind.[17]

Darwin's own assumption that his theoretical framework is not merely a description of biological processes but a prescription for social policies contributed to Bryan's disdain for the theory of evolution.

In 1959, Richard Hofstadter concluded that social scientists had come to the consensus that the biological theory of evolution does not provide a normative framework for social analysis. Perhaps Bryan would have been less troubled by Darwin's theory if he had anticipated Hofstadter's claim "that such biological ideas as the 'survival of the fittest' . . . are utterly useless in attempting to understand society; that the life of man in society, while it is incidentally a biological fact, has characteristics that are not reducible to biology and must be explained in the distinctive terms of cultural analysis."[18] By making such distinctions, Hofstadter and others are able to affirm the value of Darwin's contributions while simultaneously recognizing its limitations.[19]

FROM THE NEW DEAL TO THE NEW CHRISTIAN RIGHT

Although William Jennings Bryan may deserve some credit for undermining the Social Darwinism implicit in the *laissez faire* theories of the nineteenth century, his views would remain those of a prophetic minority until the Great Depression precipitated a paradigm shift in American thinking about poverty. With the Great Depression, the traditional response of simply blaming the poor for their own poverty was no longer credible. Private philanthropy, moreover, proved no match for the market failures of unbridled capitalism. White, Southern Evangelicals became an important part of the Democratic Party's New Deal coalition:

The first academic studies of public opinion and party allegiance, published in the 1940s and 1950s, confirmed what southern election returns had suggested—that white Southern Baptists were disproportionately attached to the Democratic Party and much more prone than other groups to support government programs of economic security.[20]

While New Deal programs did not provide full employment or eliminate poverty, they provided a safety net for the poorest of the poor and helped to ease social tensions between rich and poor Americans.

Through the mid-1960s, all U.S. presidents, including Dwight D. Eisenhower, the only Republican elected to America's highest office in this time period, would continue to expand the welfare system. The "War on Poverty" and the promise of a "Great Society" in the 1960s, however, would precipitate another shift in the public's attitude toward the relationship between government and economics. As John F. Kennedy and Lyndon B. Johnson intensified America's assault on poverty, a choir of liberal religious leaders promised that we could create heaven on earth, if only America's more comfortable citizens would pay higher taxes in order to lift America's poor out of poverty. By these standards, of course, any political platform is bound to fail.

In 1968, Americans elected a Republican. As politics is the art of the possible, Richard Nixon did not win this election by rejecting the war on poverty, though he did propose to expand the welfare state at a slower rate than his Democratic opponent. Nevertheless, Nixon's proposed "Family Assistance Act," a piece of compromise legislation drafted with Domestic Policy Advisor Daniel Patrick Moynihan, would have replaced Aid to Families with Dependent Children (AFDC) by providing a federally guaranteed minimum income that extended benefits to the working poor, eliminated the eligibility requirement that a house be without a father, provided federal support for job training and child care, and required able-bodied recipients to work or engage in job training. Nixon's Family Assistance Act would have provided a greater redistribution of wealth than any means-tested program that has actually been implemented in the United States.[21] Republican critics argued that it provided too many carrots and not enough sticks. Democrats dismissed this plan when studies indicated that a modified AFDC would be far more efficient at reaching the "truly needy" than the Family Assistance Act.[22] Among those Americans who would have benefited from a negative income tax are not just the poor, but college students whose parents are wealthy, housewives whose husbands have a sufficient income to support a family, and others who have access to wealth despite having a low income. Neither liberals nor conservatives had envisioned this type of wealth distribution. Therefore, the Senate Finance Committee defeated the bill.

Issues of poverty and social policy would move to the periphery of public policy debates until 1976 when Americans elected a Democrat, Jimmy Carter, who sought to expand welfare and health care programs. As the first Evangelical to win the presidency in recent history, Evangelicals had rallied behind him.[23] Despite his own personal piety, Jimmy Carter cited the separation of church and state to explain why he supported a *laissez faire* approach to issues such as abortion and homosexuality. Although he claimed that such practices conflicted with his own personal views, he argued that government should not try to legislate morality. Many Evangelicals felt betrayed.

At the same time, Carter would present powerful theological arguments to explain why comfortable Americans had a moral duty to provide universal access to health care, to expand welfare programs, and to promote international peace.[24] Though President Carter, quite frankly, had been unable to convert his more progressive ideas into legislation, his social philosophy would, nonetheless, be held responsible for the plight of the American economy. By all accounts, double-digit inflation and unemployment rates demonstrated that the Keynesian model of economics did not provide a sufficient guide for eliminating stagflation.[25] As many hardworking Americans saw the value of their savings and their incomes decline or, in more serious cases, lost their jobs, they felt an understandable resentment against the poor who could contribute to the common good but seemed to have no shame in choosing to live off the labor of others. In this context, many Americans were ready to reevaluate the New Deal coalition that had shaped American economic policy for half of the twentieth century.

Meanwhile, the National Council of Churches, the Roman Catholic Church, African American churches, and the Religious Action Center of Reform Judaism had successfully identified religion and morality with issues of social justice in ways that, to varying degrees, implied support for the Democratic Party. Though these communities are discussed in greater detail in later chapters, it is important to point out that many Evangelicals did not want the public to perceive that these pronouncements represented their views.

At the same time, the Republican Party was concerned that images of Richard Nixon's Watergate scandal, rather than Abraham Lincoln's Gettysburg Address, filled the minds of many American voters. The Republican Party needed a moral boost. While prohibiting abortion and legislating morality did not fit well with the libertarian themes of the Republican Party, the ability to identify their platforms with religion and morality were crucial to electoral success.[26] Over time, the Republican Party and the New Christian Right would both be transformed by this alliance.

Neither the New Christian Right nor the Republican Party had yet provided a sufficient rebuttal to the religious liberals who had persuaded most of the American public that they had a moral duty to meet the basic needs of the poor and that federal government programs provided the most realistic means for accomplishing this goal. Common enemies united the Republican Party and the emerging Christian Right, but they did not yet have a comprehensive paradigm for explaining why government programs for the poor could do no good while government legislation of morality could do no harm. The success of the Reagan revolution, in part, is that it provided a new paradigm for conceptualizing the relationship between morality and economics. Jesse Helms, Jerry Falwell, Timothy LaHaye, and Richard DeVos had already articulated key features of this new paradigm, but George Gilder deserves special attention. Not only was his *Wealth and Poverty* popular among New Christian Right activists, it was "treated as a veritable bible by the Reagan Administration."[27]

Despite the fact that Ronald Reagan was divorced, a product of Hollywood, and not an avid churchgoer, he became the next great hope of the New Christian Right, in large part, because he was willing to legislate family values (opposition to abortion and homosexuality on the one hand and support for tough crime bills and support for religious education on the other). With respect to economics, however, Ronald Reagan's presidency marked a turning point in U.S. history. His presidency provided the first direct challenge to what seemed like an ever-expanding welfare state since the 1930s. Although Reagan was not able to eliminate (or even significantly reduce) welfare spending during his presidency, most public policy debates in the wake of the Reagan revolution are couched in terms of the problem of welfare rather than the problem of poverty.[28]

SOCIAL DARWINISM IN THE NEW CHRISTIAN RIGHT

In order to understand the influence of Social Darwinism upon contemporary Christian Evangelicals,[29] we must recognize that leaders of some organizations, like the Institute for Christian Economics, Focus on the Family, and Concerned Women for America, do explicitly appeal to Darwin, Sumner, and/or sociobiology. The leaders of other organizations, such as the Christian Freedom Foundation, may advocate policies that merely resonate with Social Darwinism. Organizations like the Christian Coalition try to appeal to a wide range of individuals. Some leaders in the Christian Coalition can be identified as Social Darwinists, but the majority of their constituents are better described as economic libertarians who reject the notion that the government can effectively and efficiently help the poor while simultaneously affirming that they have a personal responsibility to meet the needs of their neighbors through private charity. Finally, those organizations like the National Association of Evangelicals and the Baptist Joint Committee that, for lack of a better term, represent the Old Christian Right continue to resist Social Darwinism and attempt to avoid the partisan politics of the contemporary culture wars.[30] While the traditional perspectives of the National Association of Evangelicals continue to reflect the views of most American Evangelicals,[31] the rest of this chapter will elaborate upon the New Christian Right's paradigm for reconciling Social Darwinism with Christianity.

The Fall Necessitates the Subsequent Struggle for Survival

It is hardly surprising that Christian Evangelicals should appeal to the story of Adam and Eve's Fall from the Garden of Eden to explain their views of the cosmos. Invariably, Christian Social Darwinists, however, explain that the significance of this story is to validate the conclusion that we live in a dog-eat-dog world where compassion is neither feasible nor desirable.[32] Opposition to all forms of economic redistribution is rooted in this interpretation of the Fall. According to Gary North, Founder of the Institute for Christian Economics, "The earth is cursed. In short, God has imposed scarcity."[33]

Nowhere is Christian Social Darwinism embodied more clearly than in the Institute for Christian Economics. They prefer the acronym "ICE," which reflects their "tough love" approach to the poor. As they solicit money for their organization, they describe it as follows:

The perspective of those associated with the ICE is straightforwardly conservative and pro–free market. . . . For well over half a century, the loudest voices favoring Christian social action have been outspokenly pro–government intervention. . . . We have to convince the liberal-leaning evangelicals of the biblical nature of the free market system.[34]

Though this initial description may sound libertarian, the works of Gary North, George Grant, David Chilton, and others associated with the ICE clarify that this organization opposes all forms of wealth redistribution to the poor, including private charity.[35]

The Free Market Is the State of Nature

If scarcity, competition, and the struggle for survival are the natural consequences of the Fall, the free market best corresponds with the nature of reality. Richard DeVos, founder of Amway Corporation and director of the Christian Freedom Foundation, explains: "Life, like it or not, is a harsh regimen in which rewards are contingent on behavior. It is a rule of life: one reaps what he sows. One accepts the consequences of his behavior: That is not an artifact of capitalism; it is a rule of nature itself."[36]

The Fall, Human Nature, and Capitalism

While their Calvinist roots dispose Evangelicals to emphasize a more pessimistic view of human nature than most Catholics or liberal Protestants, the economic implications of this pessimistic view are ambiguous. For example, Thomas Hobbes's pessimistic view of human nature leads him to submit to a Commonwealth in order to avoid the alternative, a perpetual war of one against all.[37] Marx's pessimistic view of human nature leads him to conclude that justice cannot possibly be attained without a violent revolution that eliminates the private ownership of the means of production.[38] Even the argument that government welfare programs are necessary because the needs of the poor cannot be sufficiently met without some degree of coercion by the state is hardly based upon an optimistic view of human nature.[39] Yet Christian Social Darwinists consistently argue that only *laissez faire* capitalism can be reconciled with a fallen human nature.

John Eidsmore explains, "Because of man's sin [*sic*] nature, he is basically selfish and interested in that which directly benefits him or those close to him. He is incapable of sustained activity motivated solely by altruism or the benefit of others."[40] Under socialism, therefore, people become "lazy and sluggish." By contrast, "the strength of the free enterprise system, then, is that it is based on a realistic, biblical view of the nature of man. It recognizes that for the most part fallen men will not produce, over a long period of time, unless they and their loved ones profit thereby."[41]

R. C. Sproul makes a similar argument: "Equality of material ownership may be a noble ideal in a world where sin is not present. . . . But to enforce such an equality in a world where some are industrious while others are slothful, and some are productive while others are wasteful, is not to establish justice but to destroy it."[42] Capitalism, he concludes, is the only economic system that takes original sin seriously enough to be realistic.

Rejecting the notion of a "mixed economy," Ronald Nash declares, between capitalism and socialism there is "no logical third alternative."[43] Either one lives in a society where the talented and hardworking people prosper, or one lives in a society where sloth and inefficiency are rewarded. The welfare state is simply a watered-down version of socialism.

To explain why Americans have betrayed the *laissez faire* principles of the nineteenth century, George Gilder draws attention to the liberal elites in the media, the universities, and "the Protestant churches in their group pronouncements" who have led Americans astray since the establishment of FDR's New Deal platform.[44] In response, the Reagan revolution and the New Christian Right would appeal directly to what they perceived to be the moral majority of Americans.

Gary North elaborates on the role of Christians who have embraced "anti-biblical humanism" rather than the Bible in the process of supporting wealth distribution programs:

The ethics of anti-biblical humanism has permeated the thinking of twentieth-century Christians, so that the opposition to compulsory wealth distribution programs generally has not come from Christian leaders, but has come from humanists who are defenders of nineteenth-century economic liberalism—a perspective which itself was a *secularized and Darwinian version of biblical social ethics* [emphasis added].[45]

For Gary North, Social Darwinists are his political allies. Although they use secular language, they continue to affirm the implications of Christian anthropology.

North expresses a particular disdain for theologically conservative Evangelicals like Art Gish, Ronald Sider with Christians for Social Action, and Jim Wallis with the Sojourners community who affirm liberal economic principles.[46] Gary North proclaims:

When men are taught that the capitalist system is rigged against them, that they have a legal and moral right to welfare payments, and that those who live well as a result of their own labor, effort, and forecasting skills are immoral and owe the bulk of their wealth to the poor, we must recognize the source of these teachings: the pits of hell.[47]

For Gary North, the correlation between Christianity and *laissez faire* capitalism could not be simpler: To reject capitalism is to reject God and the Bible while embracing Satan and humanism.

The Invisible Hand of the Free Market Is None Other than the Hand of God

The claim that we live in a dog-eat-dog world is somewhat qualified by the assumption that God works through the free market system to reward the righteous and to punish the indolent. Gary North explains, "*There is a God-ordained regularity in economic affairs.* There is a predictable, lawful relationship between personal industriousness and wealth, between laziness and poverty."[48] Thus, for Gary North, the invisible hand of the free market represents the lawfulness of God's judgment: Whoever challenges the justice of the free market by proposing a need for welfare programs has challenged God's justice.

Redemption in This World

The notion that God's justice can be found in this world marks a significant transformation in evangelical thought. In the religious bestseller of 1970, *The Late Great Planet Earth,* fundamentalist Hal Lindsey had preached that scriptures promised only suffering and hardship for the faithful until the Second Coming of Christ:

Jesus Christ is coming to take away all those who believe in Him. He is coming to meet all true believers in the air. Without benefit of science, space suits, or interplanetary rockets, there will be those who will be transported into a glorious place more beautiful, more awesome than we can possibly comprehend. Earth and all its thrills, excitements, and pleasures will be nothing in contrast to this great event. It will be the Living end. The ultimate trip.[49]

While many Evangelicals disputed specific claims made by Hal Lindsey, most Evangelicals from the late 1920s through the early 1970s demonstrated little tolerance for claims that the Kingdom of God can be established on earth through the political process.

Gary North's observations about the 1980 National Affairs Briefing in Dallas, however, provide insights into this transformation:

Here were the nation's fundamentalist religious leaders . . . telling the crowd that the election of 1980 is only the beginning, that the principles of the Bible can become the law of the land. . . . [T]housands of Christians, including pastors, who had believed all their lives in the imminent return of Christ, the rise of Satan's forces, and the inevitable failure of the church to convert the world, now standing up to cheer other pastors, who also have believed this doctrine of earthly defeat all their lives, but who were proclaiming victory, in time and on earth. . . . Thousands of people were . . . cheering away the eschatological doctrines of a lifetime, cheering away the theological pessimism of a lifetime.[50]

The election of Ronald Reagan thus coincided with a theological and political transformation for many Evangelicals.

Wealth as a Sign of Grace

The Gospel of Wealth is not new to the twentieth century.[51] In one form or another, the privileged classes of every Christian society have reasoned that their relative wealth, power, or prestige must be a sign of God's special affection. Yet this notion is particularly important for those who proclaim that God's hand is at work behind what appears to be the cold, random, and indifferent processes of the free market. Not all who are associated with the Gospel of Wealth, however, merit the name Social Darwinists. Many proponents of the Gospel of Wealth are libertarians who believe that the poor ought to be given assistance but disagree with New Deal advocates about the role of government in that process. The notion that one can actually gain God's favor by providing private charity to the poor, for example, runs counter to Christian Social Darwinism.

Poverty as a Punishment or Test

If the invisible hand of the free market is none other than the hand of God and wealth is a reflection of God's grace, then poverty is best understood as either a test or as a punishment. In describing poverty as a test, George Gilder advises America's poor to be diligent, patient, and to "work harder than the classes above them."[52] At another point, however, Gilder recognizes that some poor Americans are hardworking citizens. He explains that hard work does not necessarily lead to justice in one lifetime.[53] Though a definition of *karma* as justice—not in one lifetime but justice from one lifetime to the next—provides legitimation for the caste system in traditional Hinduism,[54] Gilder nowhere defends a belief in reincarnation. Rather, his implication is that today's poor should not expect to be rewarded for hard work in this lifetime, but that through hard work they can help their children to experience the American dream.

Gary North, on the other hand, prefers to speak of poverty as a punishment for sins, a sign of God's displeasure. For example, North claims that "the poverty of the Third World is the product of its anti-Christian background."[55] Explaining how the Third World's lack of faith in God corresponds with their lack of faith in the free market, North emphasizes its "*socialistic paganism.*"[56] Responding to the argument from the Christian Left that the capitalist West may be partially responsible for the poverty of the Third World, Gary North argues that such interpretations cannot be reconciled with biblical principles.[57] Though some might challenge Gary North's argument by pointing out that there are more Christians in the Third World than in the First World,[58] he would undoubtedly contend that they could not be true Christians.

The Poor Are Responsible for Their Own Poverty

To point out that Social Darwinists discount the possibility of systemic injustice may seem redundant, but the point is central to contemporary public policy debates. George Gilder, for example, claims that "the poor know that their condition is to a great degree their own fault or choice."[59]

Not long after the official unemployment rates in the United States had been in double digits, Jerry Falwell, founder of the Moral Majority, would respond to the argument that honest, hardworking individuals cannot find jobs by stating, "Generally, there are now enough jobs to go around."[60] John Eidsmore would concur: Those who do not work are "just plain lazy."[61] The obvious question arises, *Why are some people naturally lazy and others naturally industrious?* Most of the Christian Social Darwinists discussed in this chapter cite the theory of Edward Banfield who proposed that the poor have a "present-oriented time horizon," meaning that the poor are incapable of suspending their hedonistic desires for immediate gratification in order to promote their long-term interests.[62] David Chilton of the Institute for Christian Economics builds upon the work of Banfield to describe the poor as "present-oriented slaves."[63] Ronald Nash also cites Banfield when claiming that the poor have a "defective time horizon," and then he describes this condition as "genetic."[64] George Gilder identifies Banfield's analysis of poor people as an "unrivaled classic of disciplined social science."[65]

Welfare Programs Cause Poverty and Immorality

There are two common explanations for why welfare programs create poverty; the explanation that charity for the poor allows the weakest members of society to replicate themselves with children who are also unable to compete in the free market is the one that resonates most consistently with Social Darwinism. Most of the leaders in the New Christian Right are not this crass.[66] More commonly, they provide explanations for how welfare programs induce poverty by appealing to variations of rational choice theory.

George Gilder claims, "Unemployment compensation promotes unemployment. Aid for Families with Dependent Children (AFDC) makes more families dependent and fatherless."[67] Drawing upon rational choice theory, he explains that the problem of welfare is that "benefits have risen to a level higher than the ostensible returns of an unbroken home and a normal job."[68] His reasoning is certainly valid, but his assumption about the quality of life for those on welfare is dubious. Moreover, this way of framing the question leads to two options, improving the lives of the working poor or increasing the misery of the nonworking poor. Gilder explains why he opts for the latter. "There is no such thing as a good method of artificial income maintenance. The crucial goal should be to restrict the system as much as possible, by making it unattractive and even a bit demeaning."[69] Explaining how a reduction or elimination of benefits actually fosters prosperity, Gilder claims: "In order to succeed, the poor need most of all the spur of their poverty."[70]

Along the same lines, Cal Thomas, a former Moral Majority official, argues that the U.S. government provides "not a safety net, but a comfortable bed."[71] He elaborates:

The key flaw in the welfare system of the past three decades is that it has eliminated the concept of personal responsibility. If government is always there to bail out people who have children out of wedlock, if there is no disincentive (like hunger) for doing for one's self, then large numbers of people will feel no need to get themselves together and behave responsibly.[72]

In short, people could not be poor if they acted responsibly. Welfare, because it has become such a nice way of life, allows people to continue acting irresponsibly. If welfare were more demeaning, then fewer people would make this choice.

In their *Contract with the American Family*, the Christian Coalition repeats the argument that welfare programs cause poverty and illegitimacy:

The welfare system has caused the work ethic of the lowest income groups to collapse and family breakup and illegitimacy to soar. . . . This social tragedy is the direct result of our current welfare system which rewards people for not working by giving them numerous benefits and penalizes those who return to work by taking away the benefits.[73]

The Christian Coalition does not propose that those who return to work should retain benefits; rather, they propose that current benefits be reduced and/or eliminated.

Gary North goes one step further to explain why welfare programs perpetuate immorality—because they violate the commandment against stealing. He claims, "The Bible says, 'Thou shalt not steal.' It does not say, 'Thou shalt not steal, except by majority vote.' "[74] Democracy, North concludes, when it conflicts with *laissez faire* capitalism, is unchristian.

In terms reminiscent of William Graham Sumner, George Grant explains how entitlements perpetuate immorality. "To dispense the gifts of the Kingdom as an *entitlement* to any and all men without obligation—the ungrateful, the slothful, the degenerate, the apostate, and the rebellious—is to cast our pearls before swine! . . . The compassionate and loving response to a sluggard is to *warn* him."[75] Elaborating upon how compassion fosters dependency, Grant claims, "Subsidizing sluggards is the same as subsidizing evil. It is subsidizing dependence."[76]

Christianity and Trickle-Down Economics

Drawing upon the parable of Jesus' miracle of feeding the multitudes with five loaves of bread, David Chilton of the Institute for Christian Economics explains, "The Bible shows that poverty will be abolished through godly productivity and rising real wealth. The biblical answer is not, as the saying goes, to redistribute the pie, but to make a bigger pie."[77]

Gilder dismisses all welfare programs from FDR's New Deal to Lyndon B. Johnson's Great Society as misguided. He argues, "Entrepreneurs are fighting America's only serious war against poverty."[78] He claims that the redistribution of wealth from rich to poor is counterproductive. "To lift the incomes of the poor, it will be necessary to increase the rates of investment, which in turn will tend to enlarge the wealth, if not the consumption, of the rich."[79] The notion that wealth must trickle down from the wealthy to the poor is at the heart of supply-side economics. David Chilton concurs, "The man who makes the highest profit is the man who is best serving the public."[80]

Ronald Nash vehemently opposes welfare and affirmative action programs for the "least gifted" members of society, but he explains that the state might be justified in granting special favors to the "most gifted" members of society. He points out that the attempt to impose equality means that "the most gifted are forced to a lower level. . . . While each person should be given an equal chance to enjoy the best possible life, it is sometimes necessary to give extra attention to the especially gifted."[81] By taking

from the most gifted, Nash argues, wealth is not produced so all people suffer. By privileging the most gifted, wealth might trickle down to the least
gifted members of society.

Why Private Charity Is Immoral

Gary North's critique of Andrew Carnegie's philanthropy illustrates how
Christian Social Darwinists loathe private charity. North describes Carnegie
as a "devoted follower of Herbert Spencer's brand of evolutionism, with
this exception: unlike Spencer, he did not fear the effects of charity."[82]
North quotes Carnegie's law of competition to show that Carnegie understood how competition "insures the survival of the fittest in every department."[83] North continues: "So far, Carnegie sounds very much like the typical proponent of rugged individualism, or social Darwinism."[84] With the
introduction of philanthropy, however, North contends, "Carnegie broke
with the nineteenth-century social Darwinism."[85]

What Carnegie never understood was that the wealth he possessed was the result
of his enormous contribution to human welfare. . . . It was Carnegie the
"hoarder," the "wage suppressor"—in short, *Carnegie the reinvestor of profits*—
who benefited the world. . . . Carnegie the producer, not Carnegie the donator,
was the great benefactor. . . . Carnegie had served as a trustee of the masses by
his activities as an entrepreneur; he abdicated that position of trusteeship in the
name of philanthropy.[86]

North demonstrates his continuity with the nineteenth-century Social
Darwinists whom Bryan had fought so vehemently. North not only apolo-
gizes for the nineteenth-century Robber Barons (and perhaps more impor-
tantly their contemporary counterparts), he criticizes as unchristian any
attempt to redistribute wealth through charity, welfare, or any means other
than the free market.

Along the same lines, George Grant provides a new definition of "charity" so that its practice would be more consistent with Social Darwinism.
"Charity means getting rid of state-run affirmative action programs, subsi-
dies, and give-away schemes. . . . It involves getting rid of all state legislated impediments to labor: minimum wage laws, occupational licensing
restrictions, and 'closed shop' union regulation. Charity involves honest,
tough love."[87]

Not all movements within the New Christian Right share these views
about charity. While there is a strong consensus that government programs
to assist the poor do more harm than good, there is significant disagreement
about whether Christians should provide charity for the poor. The Christian Coalition, the largest and most influential organization associated with
the New Christian Right, has tried to appease Christians who support

private charity as well as Christian Social Darwinists. Although one chapter of their *Contract with the American Family* is entitled, "Encouraging Support of Private Charities," it offers no addresses to which people might send money for the poor. Instead, the contract concludes that no sane person would support our welfare system, though one *might be justified* in contributing to a private charity that predicated temporary assistance to the poor upon conversion and a commitment to change.[88] Given its assumption that the poor are responsible for their own poverty, this document hardly inspires readers to dig into their pocketbooks.

Ironically, Social Darwinists and Marxists share the same conviction that private charity is problematic, but for very different reasons. Marxists oppose private charity because they think that it makes the status quo more tolerable for the poor; thus, it prolongs if not prevents systemic changes to bring about a more just system.

Sociobiology, Not Racism, Explains Income Inequalities

Contemporary Social Darwinists tend to replicate the arguments of their nineteenth-century antecedents. In "Race and Social Darwinism," Thomas F. Gossett summarizes the conclusions of the nineteenth-century Social Darwinists by stating, "Its central idea is that the nonwhite races are oppressed, poverty-stricken, and of an inferior social status for no other reason than their innate lack of capacity."[89] George Gilder illustrates this argument quite clearly by rejecting as "false and invidious" the proposition that "racism and discrimination still explain the low incomes of blacks."[90] Assuming that the free market provides an equality of opportunity, he looks at the unequal distribution of wealth and concludes that nonwhites must be inferior.

Not wishing to be called racist, however, Gilder explains that racism is a problem of the past so that "it is now virtually impossible to find in a position of power a serious racist. Gaps in income between truly comparable blacks and whites have nearly closed."[91] One might begin to calculate how comparable Gilder believes the races truly are by comparing the incomes of whites and nonwhites. At the time that Gilder made these statements, the average per capita income of nonwhites was 67 percent of the average per capita income of whites.[92]

Despite his view that blacks are inferior, Gilder seems truly disturbed by the charge that he is a racist. In an attempt to defend why his actions are not racist, he explains that they are not based upon the color of a person's skin but by the quality of their character. If whites wish to segregate themselves from blacks, it is not because of their race, but because of their "lower-class values."[93] Relating this analysis to the integration of schools, Gilder contends, "success cannot possibly be achieved without acknowledging the prevailing facts and functions of class."[94] Defending the white

flight from inner cities that corresponded with the integration of schools, Gilder blames the "effort of some liberals to force lower middle-class families, who love their children no less, to dispatch them to ghetto schools dominated by gangs of fatherless boys bearing knives."[95]

In response to the suggestion that the character of blacks would be improved if they had access to good jobs, Gilder provides anecdotal evidence that the problems of young black men "begin long before their first rejection from a primary job and often persist long after they receive one."[96] The intractable problems of young black men cannot be attributed to racism or discrimination, according to Gilder, and their problems would persist even if they did (and do) have access to jobs.

Rousas John Rushdoony, whose Reconstructionist Movement inspired his son-in-law, Gary North, to form the Institute for Christian Economics, provides an even more powerful example of race analysis among Christian Social Darwinists. He claims:

Granted that some Negroes were mistreated as slaves, the fact still remains that nowhere in the world today has the Negro been better off. The life expectancy of the Negro increased when he was transported to America. He was not taken from freedom into slavery, but from a vicious slavery to degenerate chiefs to a generally benevolent slavery in the United States.[97]

Not wishing to be called racist, however, Rushdoony clarifies that lazy whites are like Negroes. "Today, millions of Negroes, joined by millions of slave whites, are demanding that the federal government become their slave-master and provide them with security and care."[98]

The Christian Coalition may advocate the same economic policies as Rushdoony and Gilder, but they have refrained from providing public justifications for the type of racism associated with Social Darwinism. Under the leadership of Ralph Reed, the Christian Coalition went out of its way to fight the public perception that conservative Evangelicals are racist. Ralph Reed often appeals to the image of Martin Luther King, Jr., and the civil rights movement to portray Christian Evangelicals as an embattled minority that is merely seeking a voice at the table.[99] The Christian Coalition also raised over $850,000 to help rebuild black churches that were burned by white militia organizations.[100]

Social Darwinism and Family Values

The explicit appeal to Social Darwinism occurs most often in the context of justifying traditional gender roles. James Dobson, president of Focus on the Family, "an organization committed to restoring traditional Christian and conservative family values," appeals to sociobiologists to justify his conclusion that "it is a mistake to tamper with the time-honored relationship of husband as loving protector and wife as recipient of that protection."[101] Without hesitation, Dobson appeals to scientists who draw upon Darwin's evolutionary theory to explain the biological basis of gender roles in the family:

Careful research is revealing that the basic differences between the sexes are neurological in origin, rather than being purely cultural as ordinarily assumed. . . . Both Drs. Restak and Wechsler are right. Males and females differ anatomically, sexually, emotionally, psychologically, and biochemically. We differ in literally every cell of our bodies.[102]

Dobson perceives that the social implications of Darwin's theory of evolution can and should be reconciled with Christianity to sustain the patriarchal family unit.

Timothy LaHaye, cofounder of the Moral Majority and husband of Beverly LaHaye who founded Concerned Women for America, provides a biological explanation for the relationship between the Protestant work ethic and patriarchy: "The hidden force that colors man's thinking, giving him three-dimensional fantasies and stereophonic female perception is the result of his natural ability to manufacture billions of sperm cells a week."[103] This hidden force, according to LaHaye, also "formed the basis of what has come to be known as the Protestant work ethic."[104]

George Gilder also draws upon sociobiology to explain how women's access to welfare, affirmative action, and other forms of wealth distribution undermines the traditional family. "The man's earnings, unlike the woman's, will determine . . . whether he can be a sexual man."[105] The man, whom Gilder identifies as the person uniquely qualified to lift the poor family out of poverty, finds the "compassionate state" usurping his natural role as provider.[106]

Gilder, however, does not wish to be considered sexist. He claims that men and women should be given equal pay for equal work. The problem with much feminism, according to Gilder, is that it assumes men and women are equally capable of performing the same tasks. This assumption is invalid, according to Gilder. Drawing upon sociobiology, he claims, "These differences between the sexes fully explain all gaps in earnings."[107]

While feminism is damaging enough to white families, Gilder argues, it is even more damaging to black families.[108] Assuming that academic performance and test scores, no less than the transactions made in a free market system, are based on a genuine equality of opportunity, Gilder appeals to the results of standardized tests to rank from highest to lowest the intelligence of white men, white women, black women, and black men.[109] Nevertheless, he contends that the hidden factor of male aggressiveness, understood by those who take the history of evolution seriously, helps to explain why black women should defer to black men.[110]

In summary, despite the inferior intelligence of black men, Gilder argues, black men are the best hope for the upward mobility of black families. The lure of welfare benefits, he presumes, prevents black women from accepting their proper roles. Black men, who get frustrated because they cannot have sex without high incomes, lack the testosterone necessary to compete in the marketplace. Their children, "fatherless gangs of boys using knives," will suddenly lose the aggressiveness necessary for upward mobility when they are offered their first jobs. Therefore, poor [black] families would be better off if the government did not try to redistribute wealth.

CONCLUSION

Unlike William Jennings Bryan, whose evangelicalism prompted him to criticize the concentration of power in big business, many contemporary Evangelicals, whose theological conservatism would make them the logical heirs to Bryan, see salvation as an unfettered invitation to pursue profit without guilt or shame. Perhaps William Jennings Bryan was right that the power of Darwin's theory would lead people astray! Perhaps Bryan feared that Christian Evangelicals, his own progeny, would adopt Darwin's theory as a tool for social analysis to rationalize the suffering of the poor.

The silent majority of Evangelicals in America, however, are not as caught up in the culture wars as the leaders of the Institute for Christian Economics, Focus on the Family, Concerned Women for America, and the Christian Coalition. Despite the influence of the New Christian Right, the leadership of the National Association of Evangelicals, representing the older heritage of American evangelicalism, has been more moderate in their public policy resolutions on issues such as health care reform and welfare reform. There is room for hope that Evangelicals will make a constructive contribution to economic policy debates.

If a critical mass of Evangelicals can distance themselves from the cultural warriors, explore new coalitions, recognize their particularity in the midst of America's pluralism,[111] and remain self-critical, Evangelicals may again find themselves contributing to the vital center of American culture. Such Evangelicals will appeal to their nonoptimistic view of human nature to warn against the concentration of power in big government *and* big business. In fact, it is precisely through this healthy caution toward big business *and* big government that the evangelical tradition might best serve America's political economy. If, on the other hand, Evangelicals are so afraid of embracing Marxism that they refuse to criticize the concentration of power in big business, they might consider doctrinally affirming the synthesis of evangelical theology with Social Darwinism.

NOTES

1. Robert C. Liebman and Robert Wuthnow, eds. *The New Christian Right: Mobilization and Legitimation* (New York: Aldine, 1983), 1. Evangelicals here are defined as Protestants who practice adult baptism, emphasize conversion, and affirm traditional elements of Protestant Christianity, such as a belief in the centrality of scriptures. The term fundamentalist is a narrower term referring to those who embrace "The Fundamentals of the Faith as Expressed in the Articles of Belief of the Niagara Bible Conference" (Chicago: Great Commission Prayer League, [1878]).

2. *Laissez faire* is French for hands off. In *laissez faire* capitalism, the government does not interfere with the economy. Adam Smith uses the expression *laissez faire* in his classic, *The Wealth of Nations* (New York: Modern Library, 1947; London, 1776).

3. William Jennings Bryan and Mary Baird Bryan, *The Memoirs of William Jennings Bryan* (Chicago: John C. Winston Company, 1925), 463.

4. Donald K. Springen, *William Jennings Bryan: Orator of Small-Town America* (New York: Greenwood Press, 1991), 113 [emphasis added].

5. Paolo E. Coletta, *William Jennings Bryan: III, Political Puritan (1915–1925)* (Lincoln: University of Nebraska Press, 1969), 153–54.

6. Ibid., 208.

7. Ibid., 213.

8. Friedrich Nietzsche, *Thus Spake Zarathustra: A Book for All and None*, ed. Oscar Levy (New York: Russell & Russell, 1964), 6.

9. W. J. Bryan and M. B. Bryan, *Memoirs of William Jennings Bryan*, 545.

10. Ibid., 544.

11. Friedrich Nietzsche, "The Anti-Christ," in *The Portable Nietzsche*, trans. and ed. Walter Kaufmann (New York: Penguin Books, 1954), Aphorism 2, 5, 7.

12. Note that some scholars would later identify Nietzsche's thought with Hitler's attempt to create a master race. Nevertheless, Laurence Lampert argues forcefully that such arguments are far too simplistic. See *Nietzsche's Teaching: An Interpretation of Thus Spoke Zarathustra* (New Haven: Yale University Press, 1986).

13. Herbert Spencer, *Social Statics* (New York: Robert Schalkenbach Foundation, 1970), 151.

14. William Graham Sumner, "The Forgotten Man," in *Social Darwinism: Selected Essays of William Graham Sumner*, eds. William E. Leuchtenburg and Bernard Wishy (Englewood Cliffs: Prentice Hall, 1963), 118.

15. Coletta, *William Jennings Bryan*, 552.

16. Francis Darwin, *The Life and Letters of Charles Darwin: I* (New York: P. F. Collier & Son, 1888), 68.

17. Coletta, *William Jennings Bryan*, 550.

18. Richard Hofstadter, *Social Darwinism in American Thought* (New York: George Braziller, Inc., 1959), 204.

19. Thomas Kuhn and Albert Einstein have influenced my own understanding of the relationships between religion and science. See Thomas Kuhn, *The Structure of Scientific Revolutions* (Chicago: University of Chicago Press, 1962); Albert Einstein, "Science and Religion," in *Out of My Later Years* (Totowa, N.J.: Littlefield, Adams, 1967; Philosophical Library, 1950), 25–32. Like Bryan, I would claim that

some interpretations of Darwin's theories are quite dangerous. Like Hofstadter, I would also affirm the value of Darwin's theories for advancement in such fields as medicine and agriculture. In fact, I spent eight summers working as a field technician for an agricultural company that drew upon Darwin's theory of evolution to improve the quality of corn seeds. After planting the seeds, we would subject the corn plants to various diseases, pests, and weather conditions. The seeds that performed the best under the most adverse conditions would be subjected to further tests or marketed while those that did not perform well would be discarded.

20. Kenneth D. Wald, *Religion and Politics in the United States,* 3d ed. (Washington, D.C.: CQ Press, 1997), 221. Some contemporary Evangelicals deny that their parents had reconciled Christianity with the principle of a mixed economy by explaining that support for the Democratic Party merely demonstrated distrust of a Republican Party that had attacked them during the Civil War and occupied them during Reconstruction.

21. See Theodore R. Marmor, "On Comparing Income Maintenance Alternatives," *American Political Science Review* 65:1 (March 1971), 9. Idem, *Poverty Policy: A Compendium of Cash Transfer Proposals* (Chicago, Aldine-Atherton, 1971), 57–76.

22. A study at the University of California at Berkeley by Frederick Doolittle, Frank Levy, and Michael Wiseman was influential in the committee's deliberations. See "The Mirage of Welfare Reform," *The Public Interest* 47 (Spring 1977), 62–87.

23. Evangelicals began drifting toward the Republican Party in 1960 when the Democratic Party nominated a Catholic. The Democratic Party's relatively higher support for civil rights legislation also alienated some Evangelicals. Finally, the rising socioeconomic status of Evangelicals might help to explain some movement toward the Republican Party. See Wald, *Religion and Politics in the United States,* 221–22.

24. For example, see Jimmy Carter, "Can Religious Faith Promote Peace?" in *Theology, Politics, and Peace,* ed. Theodore Runyon (Maryknoll, N.Y.: Orbis Books, 1989), 3–9.

25. For deeper insights into the theories of John Maynard Keynes that have dominated economic thought throughout much of the New Deal era, see his *The General Theory of Employment, Interest, and Money* (New York: Harcourt, Brace, 1935). For the most influential critique of Keynesian economics from a free market perspective, see Milton Friedman and Rose Friedman, *Free to Choose* (New York: Harcourt, Brace, Jovanovich, 1980).

26. For deeper insights into the relationship between Republican strategists and New Christian Right organizers, see Liebman and Wuthnow, *New Christian Right,* 24–30. Also note Duane Murray Oldfield, *The Right and the Righteous: The Christian Right Confronts the Republican Party* (Westport, Conn.: Rowman & Littlefield, 1996). Also see Michael Isikoff, "The Robertson Right and the Grandest Conspiracy," *The Washington Post* (11 October 1992), C2.

27. Liebman and Wuthnow, *New Christian Right,* 23. See George Gilder, *Wealth and Poverty* (New York: Basic Books, 1981), 3. Also note the influence of Charles Murray who draws upon sociobiology to explain poverty in *Losing Ground: American Social Policy, 1950–1980* (New York: Basic Books, 1984); Richard J. Herrnstein and Charles Murray, *The Bell Curve: Intelligence and Class Structure in American Life* (New York: Free Press, 1994).

28. Reagan stopped the expansion of welfare benefits and significantly changed the public policy debates, but his Omnibus Budget Reconciliation Act and Family Support Act had marginal effects on the welfare state. On the other hand, the Earned Income Tax Credit was expanded under Reagan. For a more critical analysis of the legislative debates on welfare reform at this time, see Robert Emme Long, ed., *The Welfare Debate* (New York: H. W. Wilson, The Reference Shelf, 61, no. 3, 1989).

29. While up to 40 percent of the U.S. population identifies themselves as born-again Evangelicals, Fowler and Hertzke conclude that perhaps 15 percent of the white U.S. population sympathizes with the theological and political agenda of the New Christian Right. See Robert Booth Fowler and Allen D. Hertzke, *Religion and Politics in America: Faith, Culture, and Strategic Choices* (Boulder: Westview, 1995), 36, 134. For further insights into the New Christian Right, see Michael Lienesch, *Redeeming America: Piety and Politics in the New Christian Right* (Chapel Hill: University of North Carolina Press, 1993).

30. For more information about the National Association of Evangelicals, including a list of affiliated denominations, see their website: http://www.nae.net/. For more information about the Baptist Joint Committee, see their website: http://www.bjcpa.org/.

31. See Chapters 4 and 6.

32. An adequate interpretation of evolutionary theory would note cooperation as well as competition. The notion of dogs eating other dogs for no reason actually makes no sense from an evolutionary perspective. See Robert R. Gottfried, *Economics, Ecology, and the Roots of Western Faith* (Lanham, Md.: Rowman & Littlefield, 1995), 12–16.

33. Gary North, *Unconditional Surrender: God's Program for Victory* (Tyler, Tex.: Institute for Christian Economics, 1981), 147.

34. Gary North, "What is the ICE?" (Tyler, Tex.: I.C.E. Freebooks), URL: http://entrewave.com/freebooks/whatsice.htm (Accessed 26 October, 1999). The Institute for Christian Economics has posted over 35,000 pages of information on the World Wide Web (www.freebooks.com). They write about infiltrating other organizations like the Christian Coalition.

35. The Institute for Christian Economics published 85 books with $66,000 in book sales for 1997. They have distributed over 800 issues of their newsletters for up to 5000 subscribers per issue. This information was self-reported to the author through an E-mail message from Gary North on May 19, 1998.

36. Richard M. DeVos and Charles Paul Conn, *Believe!* (Old Tappan, N.J.: Spire Books, 1976), 54.

37. Thomas Hobbes, *Leviathan,* ed. C. B. Macpherson (New York: Viking Penguin, Inc., 1968), 223–28.

38. See Karl Marx, "The Communist Manifesto," in *The Marx-Engels Reader,* ed. Robert C. Tucker (New York: W. W. Norton, 1978, 1972), 469–500. This text also demonstrates, however, that Marx assumes human beings can act benevolently to promote the common good with little concern for their own interests after the revolution.

39. Reinhold Niebuhr provides a powerful example of this argument. See Chapter 2.

40. John Eidsmore, *God and Caesar: Biblical Faith and Political Action* (Westchester, Ill.: Crossways Books, 1984), 109.

41. Ibid.

42. R. C. Sproul, *Money Matters: Making Sense of the Economic Issues That Affect You* (Wheaton, Ill.: Tyndale House Publishers, 1985), 117. Jerry Falwell, founder of the Moral Majority, provides a slightly different justification. In the context of discussing the Cold War, he says, "The free enterprise system is clearly outlined in the Book of Proverbs in the Bible." See Jerry Falwell, *Listen America* (New York: Bantam Books, 1981; Doubleday, 1980) 12.

43. Ronald H. Nash, *Social Justice and the Christian Church* (Milford, Mich.: Mott Media, 1983), 103.

44. George Gilder, *Wealth and Poverty* (New York: Basic Books, 1981), 135.

45. Gary North, *The Sinai Strategy: Economics and the Ten Commandments* (Tyler, Tex.: Institute for Christian Economics, 1986), 208.

46. For insights into theologically conservative but economically liberal Evangelicals, see Ronald J. Sider, *Rich Christians in an Age of Hunger: A Biblical Study* (New York: Paulist Press, 1977); Jim Wallis, *Who Is My Neighbor? Economics as if Values Matter: A Study Guide from the Editors of Sojourners* (Washington, D.C.: Sojourners, 1994); Idem, *Who Speaks for God? An Alternative to the New Christian Right: A New Politics of Compassion, Community, and Civility* (New York: Delacorte Press, 1996).

47. North, *Sinai Strategy*, 143.

48. Ibid., 141.

49. Hal Lindsey, *The Late Great Planet Earth* (Grand Rapids: Zondervan, 1970), 137.

50. Quoted in Liebman and Wuthnow, *New Christian Right,* 136.

51. The Gospel of Wealth has emerged in the wake of Max Weber's flattering argument that the Calvinist work ethic was necessary for the creation of capital and capitalism. Neo-Calvinists see the "invisible hand of God" rewarding the righteous and punishing the unrighteous. For more insight into the Gospel of Wealth, see the following six books: Neil Eskelin, *Yes Yes Living in a No No World* (Plainfield, N.J.: Logos International, 1980); Michael Fries and C. Holland Taylor, *A Christian Guide to Prosperity* (Oakland, Calif.: Communications Research, 1984); Napoleon Hill, *Grow Rich—With Peace of Mind* (Greenwich, Conn.: Hawthorn, 1967); George Otis, *God, Money, and You* (Van Nuys, Calif.: Bible Voice, 1975); Mark Yarnell, *Self-Wealth: Creating Prosperity, Serenity, and Balance in Your Life* (New Orleans, Paper Chase Press, 1999), Zig Ziglar, *Confessions of a Happy Christian* (Gretna, La.: Pelican Publishing Company, 1978).

52. Gilder, *Wealth and Poverty*, 68.

53. Ibid., 266.

54. See *The Laws of Manu,* trans. G. Buhler (Delhi: Motilal Banarsidass, 1964). Yet even the vaisyas, members of the merchant caste, are warned that they will go down in the caste system if they acquire wealth for the purpose of personal consumption. On the other hand, they are told that they will move up in the caste system in their next lives, or possibly even attain moksha (enlightenment/heaven), if they work diligently to improve the standard of living for the entire community.

55. Gary North, *Political Polytheism: The Myth of Pluralism* (Tyler, Tex.: Institute for Christian Economics, 1989), 215.

56. North, *Sinai Strategy*, 214.

57. Ibid.

58. In 1996, there were about 300,000 more Christians in the Third World than in the First World. See the *1997 Britannica Book of the Year.*

59. Gilder, *Wealth and Poverty,* 90.

60. Jerry Falwell, *Listen, America!* (Garden City, N.Y.: Doubleday and Company, 1980), 78.

61. Eidsmore, *God and Caesar,* 105.

62. Edward Banfield, *The Unheavenly City Revisited* (Boston: Little, Brown & Co., 1974).

63. David Chilton, *Productive Christians in an Age of Guilt-Manipulators: A Biblical Response to Ronald J. Sider* (Tyler, Tex.: Institute for Christian Economics, 1981), 222. One should not draw the conclusion from Chilton's title that inspiring guilt is somehow un-Christian. In fact, Chilton wants the poor to feel guilty for their sloth, feminists for their desire to be equal to men, African Americans for their desire to be granted "special favors" through Affirmative Action, unionists for their desire to steal from their employers, and anyone who desires to have sex outside the bonds of holy (monogamous, heterosexual) matrimony. In short, guilt is only evil when it is directed against the faithful capitalist.

64. Ronald H. Nash, *Poverty and Wealth: The Christian Debate over Capitalism* (Westchester, Ill.: Crossways Books, 1986), 172.

65. Gilder, *Wealth and Poverty,* 70.

66. Some illustrations of this perspective will be provided by George Gilder and Rousas John Rushdoony in their discussion of race analysis.

67. Gilder, *Wealth and Poverty,* 111.

68. Ibid., 118.

69. Ibid., 117.

70. Ibid., 118.

71. Cal Thomas, "The Clinton Plan, Welfare as We Hate It," *The Denver Post* (19 June 1994), D4.

72. Ibid. Explaining the scope of the problem, Jerry Falwell expounds, "Our nation's growing welfare system alone threatens our country with bankruptcy." See Falwell, *Listen America!,* 11.

73. Christian Coalition, *Contract with the American Family: A Bold Plan by the Christian Coalition to Strengthen the Family and Restore Common-Sense Values* (Nashville: Moorings, 1995), 86.

74. Gary North, "Free Market Capitalism," in *Wealth & Poverty: Four Christian Views of Economics,* ed. Robert G. Clouse (Downers Grove, Ill.: InterVarsity Press, 1984).

75. Grant, *Shadow,* 55. George Parkin Grant, In the Shadow of Plenty: The Biblical Blueprint for Welfare (Ft. Worth, Tex.: Dominion Press; Nashville, Tenn.: Thomas Nelson, 1986).

76. Ibid., 56.

77. Chilton, *Productive Christians,* 242.

78. Gilder, *Wealth and Poverty,* 83.

79. Ibid., 67.

80. Chilton, *Productive Christians,* 126.

81. Nash, *Social Justice,* 37.

82. North, *Sinai Strategy,* 106.

83. Ibid.

84. Ibid.

85. Ibid., 106.

86. Ibid., 108.

87. George Grant, *Bringing in the Sheaves: Transforming Poverty into Productivity* (Brentwood, Tenn.: Wolgemuch & Hyatt, 1988).

88. Christian Coalition, *Contract with the American Family*, 87.

89. Thomas F. Gossett, "Race and Social Darwinism," in *Race: The History of an Idea in America* (New York: Schocken Books, 1963), 173.

90. Gilder, *Wealth and Poverty*, 66.

91. Ibid., 128.

92. Estimated from U.S. Bureau of the Census, "Money Income of Household, Families, and Persons in the United States: 1982," in *Current Population Reports*, Series P-60, No. 142 (Washington, D.C.: U.S. G.P.O., 1984), Table 49, 166–69.

93. Gilder, *Wealth and Poverty*, 90.

94. Ibid., 91.

95. Ibid., 91.

96. Ibid., 142.

97. Rousas John Rushdoony, *Politics of Guilt and Pity* (Fairfax: Thoburn Press, 1978), 19. While Rushdoony originally made this statement in 1978, the Christian Reconstructionists continue to post this quotation on the World Wide Web (www.serv.com/thibodep/cr/negro.htm).

98. Ibid., 28.

99. See Ralph Reed, *After the Revolution: How the Christian Coalition Is Impacting America* (Dallas: Word, 1996). Reed's attempt to portray Evangelicals as victims of discrimination is reinforced by survey results that describe public opinion toward religious conservatives. See Louis Bolce and Gerald De Maio, "Religious Outlook, Culture War Politics, and Antipathy toward Christian Fundamentalists," *Public Opinion Quarterly* 63 (Spring 1999), 29. To better understand the tension within the Christian Coalition between those who seek to restore Christian America and those who seek a voice in a pluralistic America, see Justin Watson, *The Christian Coalition: Dreams of Restoration, Demands for Recognition* (New York: St. Martin's Press, 1997).

100. See Clarence Page, "Christian Coalition Trying to Heal Racial Divide," *The Houston Chronicle* (2 March 1997, 2 STAR Edition), Outlook, 3.

101. James C. Dobson, *Straight Talk to Men and Their Wives* (Dallas: Word Publishing, 1991), 168. In constructing his arguments, Dobson appeals extensively to George Gilder's *Sexual Suicide* (New York: Quadrangle/New York Times Book Co., 1973).

102. Ibid., 160–62.

103. Tim LaHaye, *Understanding the Male Temperament* (Old Tappan, N.J.: Fleming H. Revell Company, 1977), 30.

104. Tim LaHaye, *Sex Education Is for the Family* (Grand Rapids: Zondervan, 1985), 197.

105. Gilder, *Wealth and Poverty*, 87.

106. Ibid., 115. On a related issue, Gilder and others also identify a "marriage penalty tax." For a fair-minded analysis of this issue, see David Raphael Riemer, *The Prisoners of Welfare: Liberating America's Poor from Unemployment and Low Wages* (New York: Praeger, 1988), 129–35.

107. Ibid., 137.

108. Not surprisingly, some feminists have responded to these arguments. Marilyn French suggests, "Sociobiology is evoked to challenge feminist assertions of human equality," in *The War Against Women* (New York: Summit Books, 1992), 122. Carol Tavris provides a critical framework for understanding the political agenda of some sociobiologists: "The basic ideas behind sociobiology [the comparative study of animals' social organization] date back to Charles Darwin, who in 1871 described what he considered to be a basic dichotomy in the sexual natures of males and females of all species. . . . That this dichotomy conveniently fit Victorian dating and mating patterns was, naturally, pure coincidence." See Carol Tavris, *The Mismeasure of Woman* (New York: Simon & Schuster, 1992), 213. Feminists like Tavris and French demonstrate that the theories of Darwin and some contemporary sociobiologists embrace assumptions that they do not share to advance a political agenda that they reject. These are the same themes that motivated William Jennings Bryan to oppose Social Darwinism.

109. Gilder, *Wealth and Poverty,* 135.

110. Ibid., 136.

111. Another subtle irony is that the contemporary culture wars may have given Evangelicals a greater appreciation for other religious traditions. For example, Timothy LaHaye exclaims, "If religious Americans work together in the name of our mutually shared moral concerns, we just might succeed in re-establishing the civic moral standards that our forefathers thought were guaranteed by the Constitution. I realize that such statements may cause me to lose my fundamentalist membership card, but I really believe that we are in a fierce battle for the very survival of our culture. . . . We need not accept their beliefs, but we can respect the people and realize that we have more in common with each other than we ever will with the secularizers of this country." See Tim LaHaye, *The Race for the 21st Century* (Nashville: Thomas Nelson, 1986), 109. In this one respect, a greater tolerance for people of other religions, the New Christian Right marks a significant advance over the thought of William Jennings Bryan.

2

From the Realism
of Reinhold Niebuhr
to the Sectarian Stance
of the National Council
# of Churches

In the first part of the twentieth century, Mainline Protestant leaders had mortgaged their claims to moral authority with wild shifts in public policy. Having been criticized for their jingoistic nationalism during World War 1, church leaders overreacted by embracing a naïve pacifism leading up to World War II.[1] Having been criticized for their Social Darwinism before the Great Depression, church leaders overreacted by uncritically embracing Marxist analysis in parts of their Social Gospel. Critics and apologists alike were anticipating the demise of Mainline Protestantism in American culture.

World War II, however, corresponded with a revitalization of Mainline Protestant denominations. Because of Reinhold Niebuhr's influence in particular, this "golden age" of Mainline Protestantism is sometimes called the "Niebuhrian Age."[2] Mainline Protestant leaders, armed with a heavy dose of Niebuhr's "Christian realism," were able to create coalitions with Catholics, Jews, and Evangelicals; to find common ground on the most pressing issues facing U.S. society; and to support the type of prudent policy proposals necessary for approximating justice in an imperfect world.[3]

People remember Reinhold Niebuhr for a variety of reasons.[4] Some know him as *Time Magazine's* "Man of the Year: 1950." This audience recalls the critical role that Niebuhr played in providing a theological justification for U.S. nuclear policy during the Cold War. Fewer remember his critiques of the Vietnam War. Still others in "12-step" recovery programs identify him as the author of the serenity prayer: "God, grant me the serenity to accept the things I cannot change, courage to change the things I can, and wisdom to know the difference." I would like to demonstrate the relevance of Reinhold Niebuhr's Christian Realism for contemporary Mainline Protestant leaders who claim to be interested in promoting economic justice.

In 1926 Niebuhr declared himself a socialist. While at Union Theological Seminary, his leadership in the "Student Christian Movement" solidified his reputation as a socialist. Niebuhr also served as chair of the pacifist "Fellowship of Reconciliation." Although Niebuhr may be better known for his conversion from pacifism to Christian realism, his conversion from Marxism to political realism was no less significant—and certainly related. He wrote an article in 1931, "Is Peace or Justice the Goal?" In this article, he concludes:

The great problem of modern society is to achieve justice without violence. The great peril for those who make this effort is the temptation to accept a peace which is less than just and to sanction types of covert coercion which are immoral even though they do not issue in overt violence.[5]

Originally perceiving public policy in terms of a tension between the quest for perfect peace and the quest for perfect justice, Niebuhr would eventually condemn both the quest for perfect peace and the quest for perfect justice as obstacles to the attainment of relative peace and relative justice.

In *Moral Man and Immoral Society*, Niebuhr evaluates public policy proposals in terms of whether they exploit "every latent moral capacity in man" and "take account of the limitations of human nature, particularly those which manifest themselves in man's collective behavior."[6] Whereas Niebuhr criticizes conservative Protestants for failing to take human potential seriously enough, he criticizes liberal Protestants, his primary audience, for failing to take human pride seriously enough. Schooled in the Social Gospel, liberal Protestant leaders thought they could establish the Kingdom of God on earth by refusing to compromise the radical witness of Jesus. Niebuhr challenges the Social Gospel notion that Jesus offers a prudent strategy for promoting justice by claiming that Jesus taught the more idealistic virtue that material wealth is empty, impermanent, and illusory. In short, Niebuhr contends that Jesus did not address political strategy. "Politics will, to the end of history, be an area where conscience and power meet, where the ethical and coercive factors of human life will interpenetrate and work out their tentative and uneasy compromises."[7]

According to Niebuhr, religious perfectionism is justifiable in its own terms, but it cannot be justified by any appeal to historical consequences. In fact, Niebuhr questions the motives of many of his contemporaries by suggesting that they are more interested in maintaining personal purity than promoting social justice.[8] Because of his critiques of liberal Protestantism, casual readers have mistakenly concluded that Niebuhr must have embraced conservative Protestantism, but Niebuhr is best understood to be a student of the Social Gospel tradition who seeks to reform Mainline Protestantism in the direction of greater realism.

Written in 1932, Niebuhr's *Moral Man and Immoral Society* demonstrates his sympathy for Marxist economic analysis while also foreshadowing his later critiques of Marxism. Consistent with Marxist analysis, Niebuhr bluntly states, "It is important to insist, first of all, that equality is a higher social goal than peace."[9] Moreover, he seems sympathetic to the Communist Manifesto's claims that nonviolent means are unlikely to achieve economic justice.[10] In fact, Niebuhr is criticizing the Social Gospel principle that economic justice can be achieved merely through moral suasion.

In *Moral Man,* Niebuhr portrays socialism as "the accepted social and political philosophy of all *self-conscious and politically intelligent* industrial workers" [emphasis added].[11] After pointing to the "world depression and the consequent misery and insecurity of millions of workers in every land" and the "dramatic success of the Russian Revolution," Niebuhr describes Marxism as the "great promise and the great peril of the political life of the Western world."[12] It is particularly interesting that Niebuhr, who would later play such a critical role in justifying the policy of containing Soviet Marxism through nuclear deterrence, had spoken so highly of Marxism and, particularly, the Russian Revolution in the 1930s.

In fact, certain passages in *Moral Man* would lead some readers to conclude that the real debate was not between Marxist and capitalist ideologies, but between evolutionary and revolutionary versions of Marxism. While many Social Gospel figures embraced a nonviolent and evolutionary model of Marxism, Niebuhr suggests, "The difference between Marx and those who have revised his creed in the direction of a greater optimism is . . . the difference between the less favored and the more favored workers."[13] In particular, Niebuhr seems to be criticizing the relative comfort of Social Gospel theologians who argued for a more evolutionary model of social change.

In a theme that would later have significant implications for Niebuhr's public policy suggestions throughout the Cold War, Niebuhr explains "that the concentration of capital did not proceed with the rapidity which Marxian prophesy had envisaged, that a petty bourgeois class, more numerous and tenacious than anticipated, was developed under capitalism, that the growing political power of labor parties forced the state partially to equalise the inequalities created by the concentration of capital."[14] Marxism as an ideology, according to Niebuhr, did not anticipate the historical developments that would mitigate some of the dangers of unfettered capitalism.

If Niebuhr originally appealed to Marxism to counter the utopian pacifism of the Social Gospel tradition, he ultimately appeals to realism to counter the utopian justice of Marxism. "If the mind and the spirit of man does not attempt the impossible . . . a progressively higher justice and more stable peace can be achieved."[15] Niebuhr would therefore dismiss the

Social Gospel idealism that had cast its spell over the leadership of Main-line Protestantism as politically irrelevant.

At the very moment that Niebuhr began to embrace political realism, however, he also became one of the most serious critics of political realism. He argued that a "too consistent political realism would seem to consign society to perpetual warfare" and warned that "an uneasy balance of power would seem to become the highest goal to which society could aspire."[16] Recognizing that allegiance to any absolute (other than to the ineffable God) represented a dangerous form of idolatry; Niebuhr concluded that a rigid insistence upon any particular ideology (including political realism) would lead to violence and oppression.[17]

Perhaps the most important hermeneutical principle for interpreting Niebuhr's work is that he perceived himself to be engaged in an endless process of self-critical reflection. For Niebuhr, prophetic politics does not mean that one must withdraw from society to maintain one's purity, nor does it mean that one exalts oneself in order to show how corrupt others are. Niebuhr explains, "To disapprove your own selfishness more severely than the egoism of others is a necessary discipline if the natural complacency toward the self and severity in the judgment of others is to be corrected."[18] It is this humility, this commitment to *self-critical* reflection, and this willingness to listen to the arguments of his ideological opponents that would allow Reinhold Niebuhr to assume such a pivotal role in American public policy debates.

Published In 1941, Niebuhr's Volume I of *The Nature and Destiny of Man: A Christian Interpretation* wrestles with a central contradiction of Marxian economic analysis. He claims that Marxism correctly identifies "the ideological taint of all culture, [but] . . . ends in a pitiful display of the same sin."[19] If all ideology is ultimately a reflection of self-interest, as Marx insists, then is not the ideology of Marxism also nothing but a reflection of self-interest?

Like the Social Gospel figures before him, Niebuhr concludes that the "anti-aristocratic emphasis of the Bible" does resonate with certain socialist perspectives, but then he counters, "Jesus is reduced in this type of thought to the stature of a leader of a proletarian revolt against the rich."[20] In addition to rejecting this Christological formulation, Niebuhr points to a dangerous political consequence of identifying God with a particular oppressed community:

A too simple social radicalism does not recognize how quickly the poor, the weak, the despised of yesterday, may, on gaining a social victory over their detractors, exhibit the same arrogance and the same will-to-power which they abhorred in their opponents. . . . But the mistakes of a too simple social radicalism must not obscure the fact that in a given historical situation the powerful man or class is actually more guilty of injustice and pride than those who lack power.[21]

Even his critique of Marxism demonstrates that Niebuhr is still more sympathetic to the revolutionaries than to those who would preserve their own positions of power.

In one of his most consistent refrains, Niebuhr claims, "Protestantism has frequently contributed to the anarchy of modern life by its inability to suggest and to support relative standards and structures of social virtue and political justice."[22] He repeatedly argues that the Mainline Protestant leadership's insistence upon perfect peace and/or perfect justice is among the greatest stumbling blocks to the attainment of a more secure peace and a greater measure of justice:

The real evil in the human situation, according to the prophetic interpretation, lies in man's unwillingness to recognize and acknowledge the weakness, finiteness and dependence of his position, in his inclination to grasp after a power and security which transcend the possibilities of human existence, and in his effort to pretend a virtue and knowledge which are beyond the limits of mere creatures.[23]

If the biggest problem facing Protestant leaders is the denial of our limits, the solution, according to Niebuhr, is to recognize our limits but not to passively accept them. By recognizing our limits and then working diligently to push our limits, we can approximate a progressively higher standard of justice.[24]

According to Niebuhr, Protestant theologians have a particularly difficult time acknowledging standards of relative justice and relative peace:

In both Stoic and Catholic theory special consideration was given to the situation created by the fact of sin by distinguishing between an absolute and relative natural law. The former represents the demands of conscience without compromise with the fact of sin. The latter stated the legal and moral necessities of a sinful world. Thus the absolute natural law demanded complete liberty and equality. The relative natural law, on the other hand, defined the necessary coercion of government, the inequalities of property and class, including slavery, and the necessities of conflict. The absolute natural law outlawed war while the relative natural law recognized it as a necessary method of achieving justice in a sinful world.[25]

In fact, Niebuhr often distinguished the Catholic just war theory as an example of a standard of relative justice that was far superior to the jingoistic nationalism of conservative Christianity in approximating peace or to the pacifist impulse of the Social Gospel tradition in maintaining justice.[26]

The Christian utopians think they can dispense with all structures and rules of justice simply by fulfilling the law of love. . . . They think they might usher in the Kingdom of God if only they could persuade men not to resist tyranny and thus avoid conflict. They do not recognize to what degree justice in a sinful world is actually maintained by a tension of competitive forces, which is always in danger of degenerating into overt conflict, but without which there would be only the despotic peace of the subordination of the will of the weak to the will of the strong.[27]

Though still sympathetic to the Social Gospel values of peace and justice, Niebuhr concludes Volume I of *The Nature and Destiny of Man* with an intense critique of the political strategies associated with the Social Gospel tradition.

After receiving considerable criticism from proponents of the Social Gospel, Niebuhr intensifies his criticism in Volume II of *The Nature and Destiny of Man*. Continuing his theme that the quest for perfect peace and justice is one of the greatest obstacles to the attainment of a greater degree of peace and justice, Niebuhr counters that his form of political compromise is not the root of all evil:

The evil in the human situation arises, rather, from the fact that men seek to deny or to escape prematurely from the uncertainties of history and to claim a freedom, a transcendence and an eternal and universal perspective that is not possible for finite creatures.[28]

Instead of claiming to have a biblical blueprint for addressing all social evils, Niebuhr concludes, "Even the most perfectly balanced system of justice in history is a balance of competing wills and interests, and must therefore worst anyone who does not participate in the balance."[29] He goes on to conclude that the Bible does not claim that following Jesus is an expedient "strategy" for transforming social, political, and economic systems.[30]

Written in 1944, *The Children of Light and the Children of Darkness* is perhaps Niebuhr's most relevant book for Mainline Protestants who desire to understand his conversion from socialism to anticommunism. As America's foremost "liberal anticommunist,"[31] Niebuhr begins to identify Marxists as misguided children of the light:

We may well designate the moral cynics, who know no law beyond their will and interest, with a scriptural designation of "children of this world" or "children of darkness." Those who believe that self-interest should be brought under the discipline of a higher law could then be termed "the children of light."[32]

According to Niebuhr, however, misguided children of the light are often more dangerous than children of darkness, for they are often willing to martyr themselves for the cause that they identify with their gods. Echoing the argument of Thomas Jefferson, Niebuhr claims that too strong of a correlation between the will of God and any particular political platform leads to fanaticism. Echoing the argument of Roger Williams, Niebuhr claims that too strong of a correlation between the will of God and any particular political platform leads to idolatry.

While Niebuhr argues that the children of darkness represent a threat to humanity, he is more concerned with the threat posed by misguided children of the light. "It must be understood that the children of light are foolish not merely because they underestimate the power of self-interest among the children of darkness. They underestimate this power among themselves."[33] Niebuhr's form of Christian realism presumes that all people, despite their best intentions, are simultaneously children of light and children of darkness. In this "Fallen" state, Niebuhr argues, people must prudently promote their own interests without cynically rejecting the possibility of a better world:

The children of light must be armed with the wisdom of the children of darkness but remain free from their malice. They must know the power of self-interest in human society without giving it moral justification. They must have this wisdom in order that they may beguile, deflect, harness and restrain self-interest, individual and collective, for the sake of the community.[34]

Ironically, according to Niebuhr, the saint who wishes to maintain purity rarely effects social change, but the person who puts the common good before his own personal piety is likely to effect greater social change by engaging in the potentially corrupting world of politics.

Arguing that *laissez faire* capitalists and Marxists are both misguided children of the light, Niebuhr emphasizes the "similarities between classical *laissez faire* theory and the vision of an anarchistic millennium in Marxism."[35] Both, according to Niebuhr, represent ideologies that promise perfect peace, justice, harmony, and freedom. Their naïveté, however, is tragic. Niebuhr claims "there is no basis for the Marxist hope that an 'economy of abundance' will guarantee social peace; for men may fight as desperately for 'power and glory' as for bread."[36]

Marxism, according to Niebuhr, is a dangerous ideology not so much because of Marx's critiques of religion, but ironically, because of Marx's idealistic vision of a world with perfect justice and consequent peace. According to Niebuhr's historical reconstruction, furthermore, early Christianity was not concerned with property rights.

If both orthodox Catholicism and orthodox Protestantism tended to give a more and more uncritical justification of property, in which the early Christian scruples were forgotten, the sectarian Christianity of the sixteenth and seventeenth centuries, in which social revolt was combined with religious rebellion against feudalism, laid the foundation for the property ethic which finally culminated in the Marxist theory.[37]

In other words, the Social Gospel theologians were attracted to elements of Marxian economic analysis precisely because the socialist utopia was shaped by a particular conception of the Kingdom of God on earth.

After identifying a moral equivalence between the competing ideologies of the United States and the Soviet Union, Niebuhr argues that American institutions are worth defending, not because God is a *laissez faire* capitalist in a battle against atheistic Marxists, but because American institutions are more democratic than capitalistic. According to Niebuhr, "Democracy is a method of finding proximate solutions for insoluble problems."[38] This process of give and take, of compromise, of seeking unity in diversity is responsible for the rise of labor unions, social welfare programs, and other institutions that mitigate the negative consequences of the ideology of bourgeoisie capitalism. According to Niebuhr,

It is a tragic fact that the civil war [between capitalist and Marxist ideologues] which threatens democratic communities, has been created by two schools of foolish children of light, each of which failed to recognize the corruption of particular interest in ostensibly universal social ideals.[39]

While the ideologies of bourgeoisie capitalism and Marxism may be equally misguided, according to Niebuhr, Russia poses a greater threat to world peace and justice because of its undemocratic structures.[40]

The tendency toward self-righteousness is accentuated in Russia by the absence of democratic institutions through which, in other nations, sensitive minorities may act as the conscience of the nation and subject its actions and pretensions to criticism. . . . The so-called democratic and "Christian" nations have a culture which demands self-criticism in principle; and institutions which make it possible in practice.[41]

In short, Niebuhr's criticism of Russia and subsequent support for a policy of containment through nuclear deterrence cannot be interpreted as an attempt to identify Christianity with *laissez faire* capitalism. In fact, Niebuhr seemed committed to supporting democratic institutions in the United States despite the rhetoric of *laissez faire* capitalism.

Niebuhr's conversion from socialism to political realism parallels his conversion from pacifism to political realism. His most passionate critiques of Marxism come as he struggles with his own commitment to Marxism. Even as late as World War II, he perceived the communist experiment in Russia through optimistic lenses. It was not until he actually went to Germany after World War II that he began to advocate a policy of containment. For the rest of his life, he would seek a middle way between those who argued for a naïve policy of isolationism and those who argued for an all-out war to roll back the forces of communism. Anticipating that the Soviet system would collapse of its own inconsistencies, he justified nuclear deterrence as a tragic but necessary form of containment in the meantime. From 1945 to 1952, Niebuhr wrote over 100 essays justifying Soviet containment.[42] Having spurned his identification as a Marxist and a pacifist, Reinhold Niebuhr played a leading role in forging the vital center that shaped U.S. public policy throughout the Cold War.

In 1952, Reinhold Niebuhr wrote *The Irony of American History.* In this book, he argues, "Our success in establishing justice and insuring domestic tranquility has exceeded the characteristics of a bourgeois culture."[43] He argues that while the American creed sounds bourgeois, the practice is far more democratic and pragmatic. Labor unions help to establish a measure of justice for the common worker. Public education, welfare programs, graduated income taxes, and other pragmatic reforms have helped to foil Marxist predictions about the collapse of capitalism:

In this debate between errors, or between half-truth and half-truth, America is usually completely on the side of the bourgeois credo in theory; but in practice it has achieved balances of power in the organization of social forces and a consequent justice which has robbed the Marxist challenge of its sting.[44]

According to Niebuhr, the United States has developed "social programs that are wiser than its creed."[45]

Along these same lines, Niebuhr argues that it is a mistake to identify the Cold War as an ideological battle between the bourgeois creed of the United States and the communist creed of the Soviet. "The triumph of the wisdom of common sense over these two types of wisdom is, therefore, primarily the wisdom of democracy itself, which prevents either strategy from being carried through to its logical conclusion."[46] Niebuhr justifies the U.S. policy of containment by pointing to the achievement of comparative justice, peace, and freedom in the United States. Niebuhr explains: "The unarticulated wisdom embodied in the actual experience of American life has created forms of justice considerably higher than our more articulate unwisdom suggests."[47]

After writing *The Irony of American History,* Niebuhr spent the last phase of his life struggling with his own commitment to political realism by articulating his harshest critiques of a "too-consistent realism." If the danger facing the United States following World War II was to invite aggression through weakness, Niebuhr feared, the danger increasingly before the United States after the Korean War was that an overreliance upon military power, combined with what other nations would perceive to be imperial ambitions, would invite a preemptive first strike:

We are not a sanctified nation and we must not assume that all our actions are dictated by conditions of disinterested justice. If we fall into this error the natural resentments against our power on the part of the weaker nations will be compounded with resentments against our pretensions of superior virtue.[48]

Nowhere is Niebuhr's critique of a too-consistent realism seen more clearly than in his critiques of U.S. policy during the Vietnam War. This man, who had done as much as any theologian in the United States to provide a theological justification for the U.S. policy of containment during the Cold War, began criticizing U.S. policy toward Vietnam in 1967.[49] By 1969, he was calling the Vietnam War "the most pointless, costly and bloody war in our history."[50] The Vietnam War forced Niebuhr to further elaborate on the limitations of all ideology, particularly the dangers of a too-consistent realism.

CONTEMPORARY MAINLINE PROTESTANT LEADERSHIP

Most U.S. presidents have come from mainline traditions. Mainline Protestants have historically been overrepresented in the norm-shaping institutions of education, government, and mass media relative to their percentage of the population.[51] Mainline Protestants like Niebuhr not only graced the cover of magazines like *Time,* but they were actively consulted for moral guidance on public policy issues. Some Mainline Protestant leaders, most notably African American leaders whose values tend to more closely mirror their constituents than their white counterparts, continue to exercise a significant degree of political influence.[52] Most contemporary Mainline Protestant leaders, however, have a difficult time having their voices heard. Perhaps the United States is a more secular society today than it was in the 1950s. Moreover, the United States is arguably a more religiously pluralistic society than it was in the 1950s: Roman Catholics, Evangelical Protestants, Mormons, Jews, Muslims, and others play a relatively more important role in shaping public policy debates. However, another explanation for why Mainline Protestant leaders project a diminishing influence upon American culture is the conclusion that their resolutions do not represent the views of their constituents. They are described as increasingly "out of touch" with their members. Many of these Mainline Protestants have hardly been "mainline." Unlike Reinhold Niebuhr, whose policy proposals demonstrated political realism, most contemporary Mainline Protestant leaders seem incapable of finding common ground, supporting relative standards of justice, and creating broad-based political coalitions that contribute to American public policy.

The term "Mainline Protestant" was coined during the modernist/ fundamentalist debates of the 1920s. Mainline Protestants were those who conceived that there is no direct contradiction between theology and modern science. They drew upon modern theories of history, literary criticism, and social science to aid their biblical interpretations, theologies, and ethics. Today, those denominations that identify with the National Council of Churches of Christ in the U.S.A. (NCC) are generally called "mainline" or "liberal" Protestant,[53] while those denominations that identify with the National Association of Evangelicals are generally called evangelical, fundamentalist, or pentecostal. Denominations associated with the NCC include Episcopal Church, Presbyterian Church USA, United Church of Christ, Northern Baptists, Disciples of Christ, Evangelical Lutheran Church, and the United Methodist Church. Whereas Evangelicals, Fundamentalists, and Pentecostals generally maintained a sectarian stance toward what they perceived to be a hopelessly corrupt culture from the 1920s to the 1970s, new leaders have increasingly shown an ability to act prudently, make political compromises, and otherwise become relevant in the real world of politics. Meanwhile, Mainline Protestant leaders have become increasingly incapable of (or unwilling to) demonstrate political realism. They are increasingly referred to as *oldline* or *sideline* Protestants.[54] In the name of prophetic politics, they have often lobbied on behalf of policies that their own constituents would not even embrace.

Following Reconstruction, Mainline Protestants tended to identify with the Republican Party while white, Southern Evangelicals tended to identify with the Democratic Party. Since the 1970s, however, evangelical leaders have increasingly leaned toward the Republican Party while Mainline Protestant leaders have increasingly leaned toward the Democratic Party. Most Mainline Protestant members are best described as *moderates*. Over the past 30 years, they have increasingly moved from solid support for Republican candidates to being fairly evenly divided between support for Democratic and Republican presidential candidates (though they continue to tilt slightly toward the Republican candidates).[55] Even though the constituents of these churches tend to be moderate, the leaders of these denominations tend to advocate a public policy agenda that moves U.S. society to the Left.[56] This ideological divide between clergy and laity in the Mainline Protestant denominations can be illustrated in two ways. First, opinion survey data comparing clergy to laity consistently demonstrate that Mainline Protestant clergy tend to stand significantly Left of their constituents.[57] Second, the Left-leaning orientation of these church leaders can be demonstrated even more dramatically by examining the official resolutions adopted by these denominations and their ecumenical organizations. These resolutions support legislation for health care reform, campaign finance reform, debt relief for dependent nations, gay rights, and affirmative action. Other resolutions oppose legislation for welfare reform, capital punishment, prayer in schools, and support for religious schools through a voucher system. Consistently, these resolutions advocate policies that are not only Left of their constituents, but often Left of the Democratic Party as well.[58]

The Mainline Protestant leadership's march to the Left has corresponded with a relative decline in church membership as a percentage of the total U.S. population. Beginning in 1972, Dean Kelley implied a causal relationship between these two factors. In *Why Conservative Churches Are Growing,* Kelley advanced the "strictness" thesis:

[T]he sectarian and theologically conservative groups have made amazing gains in recent years. Amid the current neglect and hostility toward organized religion in general, the conservative churches, holding to seemingly outmoded theology and making strict demands on their members, have equaled or surpassed in growth the yearly percentage increases of the nation's population.[59]

Though Kelley equivocates when offering advice to Mainline Protestant leaders, conservative Mainline Protestants have interpreted his work as a clarion call for restoring traditional Christianity.[60] They argue that if churches want to grow, their leaders must call for more commitment, discipline, missionary zeal, absolutism, conformity, and fanaticism while rejecting relativism, diversity, dialogue, lukewarmness, individualism, and reserve.[61]

Further research, however, demonstrates that Kelley's conclusions are misguided. Tom W. Smith undermines Kelley's "strictness" thesis by demonstrating that the single greatest factor for explaining the relative declines in Mainline Protestant membership relative to the larger population is birth rate.[62] Contemporary Mainline Protestants have significantly fewer children than Evangelical Protestants, Mormons, and Jehovah's Witnesses.[63] Theology, educational status, socioeconomic status, and the status of women certainly impact birth rates, but there is no evidence that a significant percentage of Mainline Protestants have recently switched to evangelical denominations. Nevertheless, there is evidence that fewer Evangelicals are joining Mainline Protestant denominations than had for much of the twentieth century.[64] Mainline Protestants who leave their churches are increasingly likely to disaffiliate from any organized religion.[65]

William R. Hutchison places the recent decline of Mainline Protestant membership into a broader historical context:

[F]or the oldline churches it was the higher growth rates of the 1950s that were unusual, not the relatively lower ones that set in after the early sixties. The immediate postwar period was, for the oldline establishment, a brief shining moment that is not a particularly good benchmark for subsequent "decline."[66]

Becoming more dogmatic, intolerant, and fanatical is more likely to drive their members out of the churches than to deepen their commitments.

The radicalism of the leadership may be more of a consequence than a cause of Mainline Protestant decline. Feeling that their voices are not being heard, they have chosen to speak more loudly. Feeling that American society increasingly identifies Christianity with the Right and with the Republican Party, Mainline Protestant leaders have stepped even further to the Left. The reactionary stance of the National Council of Churches is clearly evident in their response to Ronald Reagan's election in 1980.

By the late 1970s, the American public had grown increasingly cautious about what appeared to be an ever-expanding welfare system. First, Americans grew frustrated with the false promises that poverty would end if only the government would raise taxes just a little bit more. Second, double-digit inflation and unemployment rates in the 1970s prompted many Americans to focus less upon the distribution of wealth and more upon the production of wealth. Third, illustrations of "welfare queens," who apparently had no shame in living off the labor of others, filled the tabloids, newspapers, and talk shows.[67]

Ronald Reagan won the 1980 presidential election, in part, by promising a "new" solution to the "worst economic mess since the Great Depression."[68] Rejecting the Keynesian philosophy that government policy must focus on reducing inflation *or* reducing unemployment, Reagan claimed, "In this present crisis, government is not the solution to our problem; government is the problem."[69] Stagflation, Reagan argued, was a result of increased government spending, increased government regulations, and increased anxiety by America's wealth producers. Arguing that entrepreneurs, not government, had made America prosperous, he could conclude:

It is no coincidence that our present troubles parallel and are proportionate to the intervention and intrusion in our lives that result from unnecessary and excessive growth of government. . . . In the days ahead I will propose removing the roadblocks that have slowed our economy and reduced productivity. . . . It is time to reawaken this industrial giant, to get government back within its means, and to lighten our punitive tax burden. . . . We are a nation under God, and I believe God intended us to be free.[70]

Reagan's solution consisted of cutting the rate of growth in federal spending, reducing income taxes, reducing government regulations, and encouraging the Federal Reserve Board to adopt policies to reduce inflation rather than policies to reduce short-term unemployment.[71]

Reagan did not win the presidential election by promising to end welfare; instead, he promised to reform a system that failed to distinguish between the fraudulent and the deserving poor. He claimed that two of the fundamental principles that guided his budget proposals were to "preserve 'the social safety net,' " and to "revise entitlements to eliminate unintended benefits."[72] Perhaps Ronald Reagan really sought to destroy all programs associated with the New Deal philosophy that shaped much of twentieth century (as some of his friends and critics have contended), but it is more relevant that the American public elected someone who claimed that government does have a role in protecting the poor but that the ever-expanding welfare state could expand no more, that society had witnessed an increasingly marginal return on its investments in the war against poverty, and that such programs had foreseeable but unintended consequences on the U.S. economy.

Liberal religious leaders concluded that Ronald Reagan had waged war on the War Against Poverty. The National Council of Churches (NCC) issued a resolution entitled, "The Remaking of America."[73] The NCC claimed that Reagan's proposals would "threaten the vision of America as the model and embodiment of a just and humane society."[74] Arguing that Reagan's policies were nothing short of an attempt to dismantle the safety net of U.S. society, the NCC claimed that Reagan's agenda "is contrary to

the best insights of both Christian faith and the national creed."[75] Elaborating upon this claim, they would declare, "In [the Reagan] vision of
America, the fittest survive and prosper, and there is little room for public
purpose since it interferes with private gain. Compassion is a weakness in
the competitive struggle of each against all."[76] Numerous NCC and denominational resolutions continued to echo this uncompromising tone as their
leaders prayed that this would be a short setback in the progressive march
of U.S. history. Ronald Reagan reciprocated by denying Mainline Protestant leaders the type of access to the White House that they had enjoyed
throughout much of U.S. history and by granting this access instead to leaders of the emerging Christian Right.

    While the radicalization of denominational and ecumenical leaders may
not be responsible for declining *membership*, it may contribute to the
declining *influence* of Mainline Protestantism, particularly in public policy
debates. Mainline Protestant church leaders face a crisis of credibility.
George Weigel states the case quite boldly:

The churches are not perceived, by the wider political community (or indeed by
many of their congregants), as wise moral counselors. . . . The formal leadership
of the churches has to face this fact, and it has to engage a serious debate about the
ways in which religious leaders (and others, particularly the laity) embody the "public church" in the public arena. The alternative to that conversation is a "public
Church" that, in many respects, continues to drive itself to the margins of the
debate, all the while consoling itself with the notion that it is being prophetic.[77]

Although Weigel lacks sympathy for the concerns of Mainline Protestant
leaders, he states the point quite bluntly. Mainline Protestant leaders
demonstrate far less influence in contemporary America than they did 50
years ago. Who speaks for Mainline Protestantism? Where are the
Niebuhrs? The Tillichs? When the NCC issues a resolution, who hears it?

    For example, who heard the critiques of the NCC during the Persian
Gulf War? During this war that was supported by more than 80 percent of
the U.S. population, the NCC issued a series of resolutions condemning
U.S. policy:

The U.S. administration increasingly prepares for war, a war that could lead to the
loss of tens of thousands of lives and the devastation of the region. . . . In the face
of such reckless rhetoric and imprudent behavior, as representatives of churches in
the United States we feel that we have a moral responsibility publicly and unequiv-
ocally to oppose actions that could have such dire consequences.[78]

Responding to NCC statements during the Persian Gulf War, George Weigel
falsely concludes: "While the NCC claims to represent 42 million Americans, fully 65% of its so-called members rejected the NCC's position in the
Gulf [War]."[79] But members did not "reject" the NCC position. They knew

nothing about it! (Weigel is right in the sense that they would have rejected these NCC statements if they had known about them.)

Local pastors, even when they are sympathetic, rarely share NCC resolutions with their constituents for obvious reasons. The media does not take these statements seriously. They know that NCC resolutions reflect the attitudes of a handful of elites who are more interested in proclaiming (usually amongst themselves) that they are being "prophetic" than actually contributing to the common good. While the National Council of Churches could provide important contributions to public policy debates, their statements tend to offer no room for dissent, discussion, or compromise.

In contrast to their resolutions during the Persian Gulf War, NCC resolutions during the Kosovo crisis were far more ambivalent about U.S. policy.[80] Would NCC resolutions have expressed a different tone during the Gulf Crisis under a Democratic president or during the Kosovo Crisis under a Republican president? That statements issued by Christian Evangelicals such as Pat Robertson during these two crises inversely mirrored those of the NCC may provide little consolation for those who study the culture wars.[81]

During the Clinton impeachment trial, Mainline Protestant leaders focused almost exclusively upon the need for civility in politics—in essence blaming the Republicans for the witch-hunt that led to this mess—while calling for censure instead of impeachment.[82] Simultaneously, the Christian Right focused almost exclusively upon the need for leaders to serve as models of morality while demanding impeachment.[83] Would these resolutions have expressed a different tone on both sides if this had been a Republican president?

Arguing that support for a particular candidate, political party, or platform will bring about the Kingdom of God on earth may bring short-term success. Such a strategy, however, simultaneously sows the seeds of its own destruction. It raises the standards by which policies will be evaluated as well. As Reinhold Niebuhr repeatedly warned, most cynics are frustrated optimists. The neoconservative movement consists largely of people who became disillusioned with welfare, feminism, and affirmative action by looking around and concluding that *this is not heaven*. Mainline Protestant leaders must respond creatively to the legitimate concerns of the American people, not simply dismiss them.

The strategies of Mainline Protestant leaders only make sense if they believe that they are influencing political life more profoundly than they really are, or if they console themselves with the false conclusion that they are being prophetic. Yet what does it mean to be prophetic? Is irrelevance the most salient feature of prophetic politics? No! The defining characteristic of the Hebrew prophets is that they reserved their harshest critiques for the community to whom they found themselves most accountable.[84] Mainline Protestant leaders are content to criticize those whom they deem as "other," including a majority of those who happen to occupy the same nation and roughly half of their own constituents. To be prophetic, Mainline Protestant leaders must first determine the scope of the community to which they will hold themselves accountable. If the community to which they hold themselves most accountable is a liberal elite within Mainline Protestant circles, as their critics contend, then it is precisely that community for whom they should be reserving their harshest critiques.

NOTES

1. Gerald L. Sittser, *A Cautious Patriotism: The American Churches and the Second World War* (Chapel Hill: University of North Carolina Press, 1997), 16–76.

2. Mark Silk, "American Religion and its Discontents," in *Religion and Cultural Change in American History* (Harvard Divinity School, 5–8 September, 1996), URL: http://www.aar-site.org/scripts/AAR/public/silk.html (accessed 21 January 1999), 11.

3. Gary Dorrien provides a nuanced interpretation of the relationships between the Social Gospel movement, Christian realism, and liberation theology in Mainline Protestant ethics; see Gary Dorrien, *Soul in Society: The Making and Renewal of Social Christianity* (Minneapolis: Fortress Press, 1995). Although their members were overwhelmingly Republican and among America's strongest critics of New Deal legislation, the Federal Council of Churches in 1932 would advocate "subordination of speculation and the profit motive to the creative and cooperative spirit. . . . Social planning and control of the credit and monetary systems and the economic processes for the common good . . . a wider and fairer distribution of wealth; a living wage. . . . Social insurance against sickness, accident, want in old age and unemployment. . . . Reduction of hours of labor. . . ." See "Social Ideals of the Churches" (Washington D.C.: Federal Council of Churches, n.d.), 18–19.

4. Robin Lovin provides a fuller exploration of Niebuhr's realism in *Reinhold Niebuhr and Christian Realism* (New York: Cambridge University Press, 1995). Richard Wightman Fox provides a biographical account in *Reinhold Niebuhr: A Biography* (New York: Pantheon Books, 1985).

5. Reinhold Niebuhr, "Is Peace or Justice the Goal?" *The World Tomorrow* (May 1931), 277.

6. Reinhold Niebuhr, *Moral Man and Immoral Society* (New York: Charles Scribner's Sons, 1932; reprint 1960), xi.

7. Ibid., 15.

8. Ibid., 75.

9. Ibid., 235.

10. Ibid., 141.

11. Ibid., 144.

12. Ibid., 169.

13. Ibid., 147.

14. Ibid., 181.

15. Ibid., 256.

16. Ibid., 232.

17. Ibid., 234.

18. Ibid., 271.

19. Reinhold Niebuhr, *The Nature and Destiny of Man, Volume I: Human Nature* (New York: Charles Scribner's Sons, 1941; reprint 1964), 105.

20. Ibid., 225.

21. Ibid., 226.

22. Ibid., 60.

23. Ibid., 137.

24. It may be worth noting that Reinhold Niebuhr was significantly influenced by William James' pragmatism on this point and that some process theologians have identified this conception as Niebuhr's greatest contribution to their scholarship.

25. Niebuhr, *Nature and Destiny I,* 297.

26. Reinhold Niebuhr has influenced Paul Ramsey and other Protestants to formulate their own versions of just war theory. In fact, most Mainline Protestant denominations and ecumenical organizations since Niebuhr have paid far more attention to just war theory than did their predecessors, including Calvin, Zwingli, and Luther.

27. Niebuhr, *Nature and Destiny I,* 298.

28. Reinhold Niebuhr, *The Nature and Destiny of Man, Volume II: Human Destiny* (New York: Charles Scribner's Sons, 1943; reprint 1964), 3.

29. Ibid., 72.

30. Ibid., 88.

31. Russell Foster Sizemore, *Reinhold Niebuhr and the Rhetoric of Liberal Anti-Communism: Christian Realism and the Rise of the Cold War* (Ann Arbor: UMI, 1987).

32. Reinhold Niebuhr, *The Children of Light and the Children of Darkness: The Vindication of Democracy and a Critique of Its Traditional Defense* (New York: Charles Scribner's Sons, 1944), 9.

33. Ibid., 11.

34. Ibid., 41.

35. Ibid., 32.

36. Ibid., 63.

37. Ibid., 95.

38. Ibid., 118.

39. Ibid., 149.

40. Note Niebuhr's indebtedness to Alexis de Tocqueville. See Alexis de Tocqueville, *Democracy in America,* ed. J. P. Mayer, trans. George Lawrence, (New York: HarperPerrenial, 1988; reprint, 1969).

41. Niebuhr, *Children of Light,* 183.

42. Michael Joseph Smith, *Realist Thought from Weber to Kissinger* (Baton Rouge: Louisiana State University Press, 1986), 114.

43. Reinhold Niebuhr, *The Irony of American History* (New York: Charles Scribner's Sons, 1952), 89.

44. Ibid., 91.

45. Ibid., 101.

46. Ibid., 107.

47. Ibid., 122.

48. Reinhold Niebuhr, *The Structure of Nations and Empires: A Study of the Recurring Patterns and Problems of the Political Order in the Nuclear Age* (New York: Charles Scribner's Sons, 1958), 28–29.

49. Reinhold Niebuhr, "Vietnam: Study in Ironies," *The New Republic* (24 June 1967), 12–13.

50. Reinhold Niebuhr, "Toward New Intra-Christian Endeavors," *Christian Century* LXXXVI (31 December 1969), 1663

51. Ralph E. Pyle provides an analysis of Mainline Protestant overrepresentation among cultural elites. He demonstrates that Mainline Protestants continue to be overrepresented relative to their percentage of the population, but at a diminishing rate. His primary method is to look at the religious affiliation of people inducted into *Who's Who in America*. See Ralph E. Pyle, *Persistence and Change in the Protestant Establishment* (Westport, Conn.: Praeger, 1996). Plotting the religious affiliation of members of Congress from 1967 (280 Mainline Protestants) to 1997 (169 Mainline Protestants) points to a much sharper disestablishment of Mainline Protestant leadership. See "Fewer Mainline Protestants in Congress," *Christianity Today* 41(7 April 1997), 52.

52. Despite the intentions of many Mainline Protestants, congregations remain deeply divided by race. Furthermore, African American Protestants tend to be more theologically "conservative" and fiscally "liberal" than their white counterparts. See Fowler and Hertzke, *Religion and Politics in America*, 152–57.

53. For some of the historic peace churches associated with the NCC, such as Mennonites and Quakers, the expression "Mainline" might be problematic. For some of the orthodox churches associated with the NCC, such as the Orthodox Church in America, the label "liberal" might be problematic. Because of growing tensions, some orthodox communions have indicated that they might leave the NCC and the World Council of Churches. See David Heim, "The World Council of Churches at 50: Seeking New Terms of Engagement," *The Christian Century* 115 (23 December 1998), 1246.

54. K. L. Billingsley, *From Mainline to Sideline: The Social Witness of the National Council of Churches* (Washington, D.C.: Ethics and Public Policy Center, 1990).

55. Jeff Manza and Clem Brooks, "The Religious Factor in U.S. Presidential Elections, 1960–1992," *American Journal of Sociology* 103 (July 1997), 67.

56. For a nuanced analysis of the history of liberal education and its role in shaping Mainline Protestant clergy, see Conrad Cherry, *Hurrying toward Zion: Universities, Divinity Schools, and American Protestantism* (Bloomington, Ind.: Indiana University Press, 1995).

57. For example, see James L. Guth, John C. Green, Corwin E. Smidt, Lyman A. Kellstedt, and Margaret M. Poloma, *The Bully Pulpit: The Politics of Protestant Clergy* (Lawrence: University Press of Kansas, 1997), 110–14.

58. For a concise illustration of this gap between clergy and laity, see A. James Reichley, *Religion in American Public Life* (Washington, D.C.: Brookings Institute, 1985), 269–78. Though it is now 30 years old, also note Jeffrey K. Hadden, *The Gathering Storm in the Churches* (New York: Doubleday, 1969).

59. Dean Kelley, *Why Conservative Churches Are Growing: A Study in Sociology of Religion* (Macon, Ga.: Mercer University Press, 1972; reprint, Macon, Ga.: Rose/Mercer University Press, 1986), xv.

60. See Thomas C. Reeves, *The Empty Church: The Suicide of Liberal Christianity* (New York: Free Press, 1996).

61. Kelley, *Why Conservative Churches Are Growing*, 84.

62. Tom W. Smith, "Counting Flocks and Lost Sheep: Trends in Religious Preferences Since World War II," (Chicago: National Opinion Research Center,

GSS Social Change Report No. 26, February 1988; revised January 1991), URL: http://www.icpsr.umich.edu/GSS/report/s-report/soc26.htm (accessed 2 October 1998), 12–22, 59.

63. For women under 45 years of age, liberal Protestants average 1.6 children, moderate Protestants average 1.8 children, but conservative Protestants average 2.01 children. See Wade Clark Roof and William McKinney, *American Mainline Religion: Its Changing Shape and Future* (New Brunswick: Rutgers University Press, 1987), 161.

64. Smith, "Counting Flocks and Lost Sheep," 22, 53–54.

65. Ibid., 170–72, 239–42.

66. William R. Hutchison, "Past Imperfect: History and the Prospect for Liberalism," in *Liberal Protestantism: Realities and Possibilities*, eds. Robert S. Michaelsen and Wade Clark Roof (New York: Pilgrim Press, 1986), 71.

67. While illustrations of fraud in the military industrial complex also made headlines, $600 hammers were far less interesting to interview. Moreover, discussions of privatization of the military or of America's nuclear stockpiles never materialized. Furthermore, there was no public outcry that fraud in the military meant that the goal of national defense had become unimportant.

68. Ronald Reagan, "Address to the Nation on the Economy," *Public Papers of the Presidents of the United States: Ronald Reagan, 1981* (Washington, D.C.: GPO, 1982), 79.

69. Ronald Reagan, "Inaugural Address: January 20, 1981," *Public Papers of the Presidents of the United States: Ronald Reagan, 1981* (Washington, D.C.: GPO, 1982), 1.

70. Ibid., 2.

71. Ronald Reagan, "White House Report on the Program for Economic Recovery: February 18, 1981," *Public Papers of the Presidents of the United States: Ronald Reagan, 1981* (Washington, D.C.: GPO, 1982), 116–32. For an elaboration of his principles for supply-side economics, see 130–32.

72. Ibid., 120.

73. The National Council of Churches of Christ, *Christianity and Crisis* (July 20, 1981), 207–10.

74. Ibid.

75. Ibid.

76. "NCC Tackles the Reaganauts," *Christian Century* (3–10 June 1981), 632.

77. George Weigel, "The Churches in the Gulf Crisis," in *Just War and the Gulf War*, James Turner Johnson and George Weigel (Washington, D.C.: Ethics and Public Policy Center, 1991), 89–90.

78. National Council of Churches of Christ in the U.S.A., *Pressing for Peace: The Churches Act in the Gulf Crisis* (New York: NCC-USA, 1991), 8.

79. James Turner Johnson and George Weigel, *Just War and the Gulf War* (Washington, D.C.: Ethics and Public Policy Center, 1991), 52.

80. Carol Fouke, "U.S. Delegation Meets Clinton, Annan" (National Council of Churches of Christ in the U.S.A., 6 May 1999), URL: http://www.wfn.org/conferences/wfn.news/199905/3195215264.html (accessed 12 July 1999), 1–3. Jerry L. Van Marter, "Stated Clerk Appeals to Clinton for Kosovo Solution" (PCUSA News, 23 March 1999), URL: http://www.wfn.org/conferences/wfn.news/entries/2745553812.html (accessed 24 March 1999), 1–2. Daphne Mack, "Episcopal

Presiding Bishop on NATO's Bombing Campaign" (Episcopal News Service, 26 April 1999), URL: http://www.wfn.org/conferences/wfn.news/199904/3213572707.html (accessed 12 July 1999), 1–2.

81. "It's Not Our Fight: Pat Robertson Speaks on the Kosovo Situation During *The 700 Club*" (Christian Broadcasting Network, 24 March 1999), URL: http://www.the700club.org/desk/990324P.asp?text=1 (accessed 25 March 1999), 1–2.

82. "Jewish and Christian Clergy Send Letter to Senate Urging Censure: Religious Leaders Call for Swift Process that Leaves President in Office" (National Council of Churches of Christ in the U.S.A., 6 January 1999), URL: http://www.ncccusa.org/news/99news2.html (accessed January 12, 1999), 1–2. "Religious Leader Questions Moral Principles Guiding Elected Leaders" (The Interfaith Alliance, 18 December 1998), URL: http://www.tialliance.org/tia/press/121898.html (accessed 12 January 1999), 1–2. "Religious Leaders Announce National Summit on Civility" (The Interfaith Alliance, 5 January 1999), URL: http://www.tialliance.org/tia/press/010599.html (accessed 12 January 1999), 1–2. For a notable exception, see Gabriel Fackre, ed., *Judgment Day at the White House: A Critical Declaration Exploring Moral Issues and the Political Use and Abuse of Religion* (Grand Rapids: Eerdmans, 1998).

83. "A Citizen's Petition to the Congress of the United States" (Christian Coalition), URL: http://www.cc.org/projects/petition.html (accessed 12 January 1999), 1–2. Carmen Pate, "CWA Asserts 'There is No Alternative!' " (Concerned Women for America, 7 January 1999), URL: http://www.cwfa.org/library/misc/1999-01-07_sen-letter.shtml (accessed 12 January 1999), 1–2.

84. In addition to the Hebrew prophets and Reinhold Niebuhr, my understanding of "prophetic politics" has been significantly influenced by Neal Riemer, *The Future of the Democratic Revolution: Toward a More Prophetic Politics* (New York: Praeger, 1984), 93–135.

3

From Margin to Center:
Catholics in America

Throughout much of U.S. history, Catholics have perceived themselves to be an "embattled minority" within a largely Protestant culture.[1] As immigrants from Ireland, Germany, Eastern Europe, and Italy sought to assimilate into American culture, their bishops felt obliged to show that there is no contradiction between being a good Catholic and a good American.[2] Although recent immigrants from Latin America continue this process, most Catholics have fully assimilated into the mainstream of U.S. society. The election of John F. Kennedy, the transformative nature of Vatican II, and the increased percentage of the U.S. population that identifies with the Catholic Church have simultaneously quickened this process of Catholic assimilation and intensified the Catholic Church's influence upon U.S. public policy debates.

THE CHURCH OF IMMIGRANTS

John Carroll, who became the first American bishop in Baltimore in 1790, set the tone for Catholic assimilation into U.S. society. As Catholics immigrated to the United States, they generally embraced the notion of America as the great melting pot. Tensions between Catholics and Protestants, however, could not always be ignored.[3]

Throughout much of U.S. history, "public" meant "Protestant." Public schools, far from being neutral, were forces for Protestant socialization. A day at an American public school likely included a reading from the

Protestant King James Bible, a Protestant prayer, and a history lesson about the violence, oppression, and injustice perpetuated by the Catholic Church.[4] Bishop John Hughes of New York was instrumental in making Catholic education a major focus of institutional resources.

At the same time, U.S. national policies were shaped inordinately by elites from the Protestant Mainline. Nevertheless, Catholic bishops played a significant role in the local politics of communities where significant concentrations of Catholic immigrants formed a solid political base. However, there was little cooperation between dioceses, and the degree and kind of political involvement varied heavily depending upon the local bishop.[5]

When Irish Catholics poured into the United States as a result of the Irish potato famine, they were among the poorest immigrants that America had ever seen.[6] Not only did such a vast influx of immigrants transform the Catholic Church into the largest single denomination in America, their poverty coincided with increasing Protestant perceptions of Catholics as lazy, ignorant, and violent. A disproportionately high percentage of Irish Catholics filled prisons and charity wards.[7]

Despite the intense poverty of many Catholics, their bishops did not want to appear too radical or subversive because they still wanted to prove that Catholics could be "good" Americans.[8] By the end of the nineteenth century, however, Cardinal James Gibbons of Baltimore was instrumental in identifying the Catholic Church as a friend, or at least not a foe, of organized labor. He personally pleaded the case in Rome that the Catholic Church should not condemn the Knights of Labor. At a speech in 1887, Gibbons proclaimed, "The great questions of the future are not those of war, of commerce or finance, but the social questions—the questions which concern the improvement of the condition of the great popular masses, and especially the working people."[9] Archbishop John Ireland of St. Paul, Minnesota, who had accompanied Gibbons to Rome, also played a significant role in forging "liberal Catholicism."[10]

RERUM NOVARUM: THE FOUNDATION OF CATHOLIC SOCIAL THOUGHT

Further identifying the Catholic Church with labor, while vehemently criticizing socialism, Pope Leo XIII released the first of the social encyclicals, *Rerum Novarum*. In 1891, eight years after the death of Karl Marx, Pope Leo begins this encyclical by describing industrialization in terms consistent with socialist analysis:

The coming of new industrial growth with the application of new techniques; of changed relationships between employers and employed; of immense wealth for a small number and deepest poverty for the multitude . . . from all of these changes has come an explosive struggle.[11]

In describing this process of industrialization, Pope Leo XIII clearly sympathizes with the plight of the common laborers who must sell their labor (in exchange for less than a just wage) to owners of the means of production who are not equally compelled to enter this contractual relationship.

As a result of such grave inequalities, Pope Leo XIII makes the bold assertion that "the first task is to save the wretched workers from the brutality of those who make use of human beings as mere instruments for the unrestrained acquisition of wealth."[12] In describing the lives of the workers, Pope Leo XIII declares, "They are tossed about helplessly and disastrously in conditions of pitiable and utterly undeserved misery."[13] Pope Leo XIII recognizes that workers must unite and organize (in what he calls *associations*) if they are to restore the power imbalances between laborers and the owners of the means of production.

Nevertheless, Pope Leo XIII clearly rejects a socialist revolution; instead, he calls for reforms that would mitigate the negative effects of the free market. Twenty-six years before the Bolshevik Revolution in Russia, he argues that socialism is misguided for at least two reasons. First, he states that the socialist cure, eliminating private property, is unjust for those owners of the means of production who have acquired their property through legitimate means. Second, workers would actually be worse off, he argues, if in the name of justice they lost their freedom to use the fruits of their labor as they pleased.[14] If they sacrifice too much freedom, Pope Leo XIII anticipates, "all incentive for individuals to exercise their ingenuity and skill would be removed and the very founts of wealth dry up. The dream of equality would become a reality of equal want and degradation for all."[15]

Setting the stage for all future encyclicals, Pope Leo XIII sought a third way, beyond *laissez faire* capitalism and socialism. He continues by arguing that some degree of inequality in society is inevitable. "Anyone who claims to be able to rid the common people of all pain and sorrow and to bring them peace and a life of never-ending pleasure lies outrageously."[16] Yet shortly after criticizing the utopian nature of socialism, he affirms the notion that God seems to give preference to people in unfortunate circumstances.[17]

In addition to denying that poverty is a sign of disgrace, Pope Leo XIII lifts up voluntary poverty as a witness against those who would seek ultimate happiness in material wealth. At the same time, however, he warns against understanding Christianity in purely other-worldly terms. "It must not be thought that the Church's great concern with the care of souls leads her to neglect the affairs of this earthly and mortal life. She wants expressly to see the unpropertied workers emerge from their great poverty and better their condition."[18] Thus, Christians are encouraged to simultaneously recognize the inevitability of suffering, while diligently working to rid the suffering of others. Pope Leo XIII argues that material wealth cannot provide ultimate satisfaction, but that the Church has a responsibility to improve the lives of the poor.

Pope Leo XIII rejects the Marxist argument that charity is no longer necessary in a socialist society.[19] Additionally, he suggests, "The state has no authority to swallow up either the individual or the family. To the extent that the common good is not endangered or any person hurt, justice requires full freedom of action for both."[20]

On the other hand, he claims that the state does justifiably play a role in helping the poor in order to contribute to the common good.[21] "Rich people can use their wealth to protect themselves and have less need of the state's protection; but the masses of the poor have nothing of their own with which to defend themselves and have to depend above all upon the protection of the state."[22] Thus, Pope Leo XIII provides a justification for a limited role that government must play in order to approximate justice and to promote the common good, but he rejects the socialist demand for a more radical distribution of wealth.

Although Pope Leo XIII defends the right of workers to organize and to engage in strikes as a matter of last resort, he encourages states to remove "the causes of conflict between employers and workers."[23] Elaborating upon the causes of conflict, he focuses upon the long hours, low wages, and unhealthy working conditions for many workers. Moreover, he explains that contracts between those who are not equals in power may be unjust.[24] A starving person, for example, may be forced into accepting an unreasonable agreement. Therefore, he explains that a "just wage" is not simply what is sufficient to sustain one's family, but a wage that allows the worker to save money for the purposes of acquiring one's own property. Pointing to the enormous gulf between laborers and those who own the means of production, Pope Leo XIII argues that fostering a society with a strong middle class and without the extremes of poverty and wealth would diminish the potential for a literal class war.[25]

AMERICAN CATHOLIC BISHOPS' *PROGRAM OF SOCIAL RECONSTRUCTION*

Drawing heavily upon *Rerum Novarum,* the National Catholic Welfare Council, under the leadership of Bishop John Ryan, issued the *Program of Social Reconstruction* in February of 1919. While repeatedly rejecting socialism, the American bishops call for a more equitable distribution of wealth (and in some cases a redistribution of wealth) through "prevention of monopolistic control of commodities, adequate government regulation of such public service monopolies as will remain under private operation, and heavy taxation of [high] incomes, excess profits, and inheritances."[26] Furthermore, they would recommend minimum wage laws, the abolition of child labor, a national labor board, vocational training for unskilled laborers, subsidized housing projects in poverty-stricken cities, and a system of social insurance "against illness, invalidity, unemployment, and old age."[27] The correlation between these proposals and the reforms that would be enacted through New Deal legislation is quite striking!

Elaborating upon the philosophical foundations of their proposals, they identify three major defects of the present economic system: "Enormous inefficiency and waste in the production and distribution of commodities; insufficient incomes for the great majority of wage earners, and unnecessarily large incomes for a small minority of privileged capitalists."[28] Anticipating the *laissez faire* argument that profit is merely a reflection of service to the common good, the bishops respond, "The man who utilizes his ability to produce cheaper than his competitors for the purpose of exacting from the public as high a price for his product as is necessary for the least efficient businessman is a menace rather than a benefit to industry and society."[29]

At the same time that they highlight the defects of the current system, they claim that a socialist revolution would be unlikely to succeed in the United States. Rather than bemoaning this prognosis, they argue, "Socialism would mean bureaucracy, political tyranny, the helplessness of the individual as a factor in the ordering of his own life, and in general social inefficiency and decadence."[30] Despite these harsh critiques of socialism, their letter implicitly warns American capitalists that a failure to reform the current system, to minimize the gulf between the owners and the laborers, and to improve the well-being of the vast majority of American citizens could lead to such a disastrous revolution. The bishops conclude by stating:

[T]he laborer is a human being, not merely an instrument of production; and that the laborer's right to a decent livelihood is the first moral charge upon industry. The employer has a right to get a reasonable living out of his business, but he has no right to interest on his investment until his employees have obtained at least living wages. This is the human and Christian, in contrast to the purely commercial and pagan, ethics of industry.[31]

In this manner, the *Program of Social Reconstruction* would dispose American Catholic bishops to identify with a small but growing coalition of moderates who sought to reform capitalism.

A decade after the *Program of Social Reconstruction* was issued, the United States found itself in the midst of the Great Depression. Most of the reforms advocated by the Catholic bishops had not yet been enacted. The crises associated with the Depression served to embolden the Catholic bishops. In 1930, they issued a "Statement on Unemployment" that begins by stating, "Again the United States is suffering the tragedy of millions of men and women who need work, who want work, and who can find no work to do."[32]

After expressing deep gratitude to individuals "who give food to the hungry, clothe the naked, [and] harbor the harborless," the bishops call for a deeper systemic analysis of the causes of poverty and unemployment in the United States:

More than temporary alms is necessary. Justice should be done. This unemployment returning again to plague us after so many repetitions during the century past is a sign of deep failure in our country. Unemployment is the great peacetime physical tragedy of the nineteenth and twentieth centuries, and . . . it is one of the great moral tragedies of our time.[33]

This conclusion that systemic unemployment is a moral tragedy, not just an economic condition, would become a consistent principle within Catholic social teaching.

They conclude their "Statement on Unemployment" by pointing to their own *Program of Social Reconstruction* as a guide for public policy. They even make the bold assertion, "Had this passage been heeded during the dozen years since it was written, it would in itself have gone far to prevent the calamity we now undergo."[34] Clearly, these Catholic bishops do not see themselves as providing merely a short-term response to the crisis of the Great Depression but as promoting policies that would prevent such crises in the future.

THE DEVELOPMENT OF CATHOLIC SOCIAL THEORY

One year later (1931), Pope Pius XI would issue *Quadragesimo Anno,* which commemorated the fortieth anniversary of *Rerum Novarum.* Explaining the significance of Pope Pius XI's encyclical, Michael Walsh and Brian Davies suggest, "Perhaps without *Quadragesimo Anno* there would have been no modern Catholic social doctrine. *Rerum Novarum* might have been a once-off, rather than a start of a tradition."[35]

In light of violence and oppression by Russian, Chinese, and other revolutionaries, Pope Pius XI would demonstrate an even stronger condemnation of communism than his predecessor, Pope Leo XIII:

Communism teaches and seeks two objectives: Unrelenting class warfare and absolute extermination of private ownership. . . . To achieve these objectives there is nothing which it does not dare, nothing for which it has respect or reverence; and when it has come to power, it is incredible and portentlike in its cruelty and inhumanity. The horrible slaughter and destruction through which it has laid waste vast regions of eastern Europe and Asia are the evidence.[36]

The condemnation of communism would remain an important part of Catholic social teaching throughout the twentieth century.[37] Though somewhat mitigated during World War II because of the threat posed by Hitler's Nazi movement, the Vatican and the American bishops would contribute significantly to the anticommunist movement in America and abroad.

Nevertheless, Pope Pius XI would simultaneously warn about the dangers of *laissez faire* practices. He protests the great wealth for a handful of capitalists corresponding with a worldwide depression for the masses. Pointing to the changing nature of global economics, particularly with the rise of corporations, stock markets, and an impersonal banking industry, Pope Pius XI proclaims:

[I]t is obvious that not only is wealth concentrated in our times, but an immense power and despotic economic dictatorship is consolidated in the hands of a few, who often are not owners but only the trustees and managing directors of invested funds which they administer according to their own arbitrary will and pleasure.[38]

Rather than promoting the common good, moreover, Pope Pius XI argues:

This concentration of power and might, the characteristic mark, as it were, of contemporary economic life, is the fruit that the unlimited freedom of struggle among competitors has of its own nature produced, and which lets only the strongest survive; and this is often the same as saying, those who fight the most violently, those who give least heed to their conscience.[39]

Responding to the argument that *laissez faire* capitalism is the most morally justifiable type of economic system, Pope Pius XI argues that such systems have historically rewarded individuals who are immoral, willing to oppress their workers, and demonstrate no higher commitments to the common good. In light of a worldwide recession, moreover, he even proclaims that "Free competition has destroyed itself; economic dictatorship has supplanted the free market; . . . all economic life has become tragically hard, inexorable, and cruel."[40]

Another significance of *Quadragesimo Anno* is Pope Pius XI's clarification regarding the Catholic Church's teachings about private property. In response to criticism that he and Pope Leo XIII "had taken and were still taking the part of the rich against the non-owning workers," Pope Pius XI declares:

For, as one is wrecked upon, or comes close to, what is know as "individualism" by denying or minimizing the social and public character of the right of property, so by rejecting or minimizing the private and individual character of this same right, one inevitably runs into "collectivism" or at least closely approaches its tenets.[41]

Given this interpretation of the public and private nature of property, Pope Pius XI calls for a constructive tension between individual rights and the common good rather than an abolition of one in favor of the other.

Later that same year (1931), the U.S. Catholic Bishops would issue a "Statement on Economic Crisis" that would express gratitude to all who fostered private charity while simultaneously proclaiming, "we are convinced, because of the vastness of the number suffering, that federal and state appropriations for relief in some form will become necessary."[42] Placing the contemporary crisis into a broader context, they claim:

The unemployment crisis is deep-rooted in the avarice of human nature which for a century and more has caused disorganization of the processes of production and distribution. . . . We ask a living wage for the family; a proper proportion between the wages of the different kinds of workers; an ample sufficiency for all. We ask for wages that will provide employment to the greatest extent possible; and for an equitable sharing of the goods produced so abundantly by industry.[43]

In short, they insist that a more equitable distribution of wealth between capitalists and laborers is a moral imperative.

Two years later (1933), the U.S. Catholic Bishops would issue yet another pastoral letter, "The Present Crisis." Concurring with Pope Pius XI that all of humanity had not suffered such hardships since the Flood, they praised the discipline and charity of many Catholics. "Their sufferings, their privations, their generosity, especially that shown by the poor to those still poorer, will fill an inspiring page of our history."[44]

Arguing that *laissez faire* economics had no small role to play in the Great Depression, they criticize those who would hold individual freedom inviolable:

Many, having a materialistic attitude toward life, and therefore without a true moral sense of their obligations, object to any restriction of competition, even that which degrades the dignity of human labor and ignores every principle of justice. Others resent opposition to monopolies and dictatorship in the economic world, and regard as an infringement of their rights any interference with their powerful corporations, and mergers, or with lobbies, which have sought to corrupt and to control the state.[45]

While maintaining a balanced rejection of the extremes of *laissez faire* capitalism and socialism, the Leftward direction that they advocate is clear throughout this text. Describing *laissez faire* capitalism, they proclaim:

That same demoralizing philosophy defended, and defends today, unrestrained individual economic freedom and the economic dictatorship that has succeeded it. That philosophy permits individuals, corporations, and nations to accumulate as much wealth as they can, according to the unfair methods of modern business, and to use such accumulated wealth as they see fit. It honors and proclaims as sovereign rulers of economic empires men who have succeeded in amassing unjustly these fabulous fortunes. That philosophy has broken down or forbidden the establishment of protective organizations. . . . It has denied government its right to guard justice and the common good. It has given greed a free hand. . . . Such a philosophy has always been and will ever be false and unchristian in principle and application. It has literally taken God out of the world.[46]

In short, this resolution offered the harshest critique of *laissez faire* theory that had yet been issued on behalf of the U.S. Catholic Bishops.

In their corresponding critique of communism, they would indicate that the false promises of communism are a misguided but direct response to the failures of *laissez faire* capitalism. Moreover, they would warn that the spread of communism is quite possible because Marxist rhetoric of equality "is distinctively Christian in origin and purport," but then they would clarify this point by stating that "in the hands of the communists it is merely a snare to allure those who are oppressed by the prevailing economic maladjustment into accepting the iniquitous social and religious tenets of Lenin and Stalin."[47] Warning that a failure to improve the living conditions of the masses might well lead to a global expansion of communism, however, the bishops imply that owners and managers of the means of production ought to be among the most ardent of those supporting the reform of capitalist systems.

By the presidency of Franklin D. Roosevelt (1932–1945), a tradition of Catholic social thought had not only become well established, it appeared to be influencing American public policy as well. As Timothy Byrnes points out: "Virtually the entire bishops program of 1919 was eventually enacted into law during Roosevelt's presidency."[48] Although Catholics were not alone in advocating the type of policies embraced during Roosevelt's New Deal, many Catholics were pleased to see that their leaders were increasingly perceived as social and moral guides for the larger American public.[49] In the meantime, New Deal legislation further reinforced the identification of Catholics with the Democratic Party so that Catholics "generally provided more than a third of the total Democratic presidential vote in the New Deal and later eras."[50]

Although American Catholic bishops would occasionally comment upon economic policy, the number and intensity of these proclamations would diminish significantly for four reasons. First, the implementation of New Deal legislation would minimize the effects of the crises to which they needed to respond. Second, Catholics had entered the socioeconomic mainstream of U.S. society shortly after World War II and would no longer disproportionately benefit from stronger unions, childhood labor laws, minimum wage legislation, workplace safety regulations, unemployment benefits, food stamps, and Aid to Families with Dependent Children. Third, the U.S. Catholic Bishops would emphasize their rejection of socialism, their opposition to the practices of the Soviet Union, and their justification for the U.S. policy of containment throughout the Cold War. Fourth, other critical issues would demand a greater proportion of the bishops' resources.

THE 1960s: A TRANSITIONAL DECADE

In 1960, John F. Kennedy became the first (and so far only) Catholic to be elected president of the United States. At the time John F. Kennedy was

elected president, many Protestants accused Catholics of engaging in idolatry because they "worshipped Mary instead of God," of being antidemocratic because they embraced "popery," of being more loyal to Italy or Ireland because of their recent immigrant status, and being "premodern"
because of Catholic teachings on such issues as evolution.[51] Official teachings of the Catholic Church had tended to reinforce similarly malignant
images of non-Catholics. Another John would help to transform non-
Catholic perceptions of Catholics.

During Vatican II, the ecumenical council of 1962–1965, Pope John
XXIII convened the bishops from around the world with the hope of bringing the church more fully into modern times. Although the new *Pastoral
Constitution on the Church in the Modern World* would continue to claim
that the Church is in some sense "necessary for salvation," it would simultaneously claim that *Protestant and Orthodox Christians* "are in some real
way joined with us in the Holy Spirit."[52] Responding to the obvious hor-
rors of the Holocaust and the Church's own complicity in the history of
anti-Semitism, it would speak of the *Jews* "to whom Christ was born
according to the flesh."[53] Rather than insisting that Judaism represents a
defunct old covenant, they would claim that God does not break God's
promises. Reversing a 13-century practice of hostility toward *Islam,* they
would declare: "the plan of salvation also includes those who acknowledge
the Creator. In the first place among these there are the Moslems, who, pro-
fessing to hold the faith of Abraham, along with us adore the one and merciful God, who on the last day will judge mankind."[54] Demonstrating a
more tolerant though arguably still ethnocentric view of other religions,
they would claim: "Nor is God Himself far distant from those who in shad-
ows and images seek the unknown God, for it is He who gives to all men
life and breath and every other gift (cf. Acts 17:25–28), and who as Savior
wills that all men be saved (cf. 1 Tim. 2:4)."[55] In these and numerous other
passages, Vatican II fosters greater tolerance toward non-Catholics. In
return, many non-Catholics have reciprocated by discarding their own anti-
Catholic prejudices. By reducing anti-Catholic sentiment while encouraging
Catholics to work in cooperation with others of goodwill, Vatican II further
enhanced the ability of Catholics to influence U.S. public policy.

Documents hammered out during Vatican II did more than improve relations between Catholics and non-Catholics, they also helped to undermine
the argument of those who insisted that the Roman Catholic Church is hopelessly antidemocratic. Claiming that God's grace may be operative at any
social location, Vatican II also softens (but does not dismantle) the Catholic
hierarchy and diminishes (but does not eliminate) the distinction between
clergy and laity.[56] Furthermore, the Vatican gave greater authority to Episcopal Conferences with the hope that they could more effectively relate
Catholic teachings to national or regional issues. The National Conference
of Catholic Bishops, created in November of 1966, is a direct result of this

initiative.[57] This new conference could claim greater unity and greater authority than its predecessor, the National Catholic Welfare Council.

Unlike its Protestant counterparts, the National Conference of Catholic Bishops is a canonical body that maintains a hierarchical authority, is mandatory for its bishops, and claims that the collective authority is greater than the voice of individual bishops. Ironically, the organizational structure of the Catholic Church has created a council that is more democratic than its Protestant counterparts. When Protestants do not like resolutions adopted by their denominational or ecumenical leaders, they form a new denomination or they ignore the ecumenical bodies that claim to speak on their behalf. The sharp division between the Protestant Left and the Protestant Right in the contemporary culture wars is largely a result of this continued process. By way of contrast, Catholic leaders tend to work out their differences or remain in a constructive tension with the institution; thus, Catholic resolutions tend to be more balanced, nuanced, and representative of their constituents than resolutions adopted by Protestant denominations and their ecumenical bodies.

After empowering bishops to play a more prominent role in addressing public policy issues, the *Pastoral Constitution on the Church in the Modern World* also clarifies the general teachings of the Catholic Church on several issues. When identifying the parameters of the Catholic Church's position on economic policy, it states:

Growth must not be allowed merely to follow a kind of automatic course resulting from the economic activity of individuals. Nor must it be entrusted solely to the authority of government. Hence theories which obstruct the necessary reforms in the name of a false liberty must be branded as erroneous. The same is true of those theories which subordinate the basic right of individual persons and groups to the collective organization of production.[58]

Thus, the Catholic Church would reaffirm its evenhanded rejection of both *laissez faire* capitalism and communism. Popes John XXIII,[59] Paul VI,[60] and John Paul II[61] would continue to address issues of economic justice by advocating the type of mixed economy practiced by the United States and Western Europe.

FROM *ECONOMIC JUSTICE FOR ALL* TO THE PRESENT

For the U.S. Catholic Bishops, the issue of economic policy would take a back seat to other issues; that is, until the rise of the New Right in the late 1970s followed by Reaganomics in the 1980s.[62] As the attack upon the welfare state intensified, the American bishops felt compelled to respond with *Economic Justice for All: Pastoral Letter on Catholic Social Teaching and the U.S. Economy.* Their critics would argue that the National Conference of Catholic Bishops had distorted Catholic social teaching, but the relative

silence on U.S. economic policy throughout the Cold War is best understood as a degree of satisfaction with the welfare state, not an ideological
commitment to *laissez faire* capitalism.[63]

In their pastoral letter, the U.S. Catholic Bishops would elaborate upon
the sources of Catholic moral theology, the history of Catholic social
thought, and the relevance of faith to everyday life for Catholic consumers,
citizens, workers, and owners. They would claim to "write as pastors, not
public officials . . . as moral teachers, not economic technicians."[64] Their
intended audience included non-Catholics as well as Catholics. Their 183-
page document revolved around the following six principles.[65]

1. Every economic decision and institution must be judged in light of whether it
   protects or undermines the dignity of human persons.
2. Human dignity can be realized and protected only in community.
3. All people have a right to participate in the economic life of society.
4. All members of society have a special obligation to the poor and vulnerable.
5. Human rights are the minimum conditions for life in community.
6. Society as a whole, acting through public and private institutions, has the moral
   responsibility to enhance human dignity and protect human rights.

Although providing a balanced critique of individualistic and socialistic ideologies, the emphasis throughout this document is clearly a reaction to
what the Catholic bishops perceive to be an individualistic assault upon the
institutions that had provided a safety net for the poorest and most vulnerable Americans.

Elaborating upon their principle that society has a special obligation
to the poor and vulnerable, they would explain. "The justice that was the
sign of God's covenant with Israel was measured by how the poor and
unprotected—the widow, the orphan, and the stranger—were treated."[66]
Given this "preferential option for the poor," many Americans, Catholic
and non-Catholic alike, failed to see *Economic Justice for All* as a reasonable and balanced approach to economics, despite the bishops' claim, "We
reject ideological extremes and start from the fact that ours is a 'mixed'
economy, the product of a long history of reform and adjustment."[67] In the
wake of the Cold War, the economic debate had changed in America so that
support for the type of reformed capitalism associated with the welfare
state was increasingly considered Left rather than centrist, socialist rather
than moderate, unchristian rather than Christian.

Although the U.S. Catholic Bishops draw correlations between the end of
the nineteenth century and the end of the twentieth century, the biggest
change that they could identify is the globalization of capitalism. Such globalization creates certain risks for American laborers and decreases the number of jobs that provide a living wage.[68] In particular, the globalization of

capitalism encourages investors who wish to maximize profits to relocate to those nations where labor is unorganized and the state provides few regulations for worker safety, environmental protection, or welfare for the common good. In short, they fear that the globalization of capitalism could well undermine the delicate balance between capitalists and laborers, individual responsibility and social responsibility, freedom and justice that has been established through the American experiment. While the New Christian Right argues that the United States will suffer the same fate as the Soviet Union if we interfere with the free market, the U.S. Catholic Bishops argue that people throughout the world might suffer the same fate as America during the Great Depression if we fail to intervene in the free market—extraordinary wealth for a handful of individuals who control the means of production and abject poverty and powerlessness for the vast majority.

In particular, they point to the worsening plight of blacks, Hispanics, Native Americans, women, and children.[69] They also identify three trends affecting middle class American families: an increasing number of hours that a typical American family must work outside the home in order to maintain its standard of living, decreasing job security, and an increasing percentage of Americans who lack access to primary and preventive health care.[70]

At a time when the American people (including a slight majority of Catholics!) had twice elected a president who blamed welfare taxes for the inability of American corporations to compete in the global market, the bishops' analyses would almost inevitably be considered radical and partisan. In a context where Christians had increasingly adopted the libertarian principle that the invisible hand of the free market generally rewards those who are productive with wealth and punishes those who are slothful with poverty, the Catholic bishops could be seen as articulating the antithesis: "No one may claim the name Christian and be comfortable in the face of the hunger, homelessness, insecurity, and injustice found in this country and the world."[71]

In the second half of *Economic Justice for All,* the U.S. Catholic Bishops focused upon particular economic policy issues. Focusing upon unemployment, they would proclaim, "Full employment is the foundation of a just economy. . . . Employment is a basic right, a right which protects the freedom of all to participate in the economic life of society."[72] Citing statistics from the U.S. Department of Labor, they point out that roughly one-eighth of the U.S. workforce is unable to find full-time employment and that almost three-fourths of unemployed Americans do not receive unemployment insurance benefits.[73] In making their recommendations, however, they fall short of insisting that the federal government is responsible for providing full employment. Thus, the bishops' specific recommendation of holding business, labor, and government responsible for approximating full employment is not nearly as bold as one might expect after reading their harsh critiques of the libertarian ideology of *laissez faire* economics. In fact, their specific recommendations are far more consistent with reformed capitalism than with socialist theory.

Moving to the issue of poverty, the U.S. Catholic Bishops focus upon underemployment, the feminization of poverty, the dramatic increases in childhood poverty, the correlation between racism and poverty, and the increasing gap between the rich and the poor.[74] To highlight the extraordinary gap, they cite a survey by the Federal Reserve Board. "In 1983, 54 percent of the total net financial assets were held by 2 percent of all families."[75] After clarifying that some degree of inequality is not only acceptable, but perhaps even desirable, the U.S. Catholic Bishops offer several recommendations. First, they affirm their commitments to public policy programs such as the Social Security Program. Second, they debunk stereotypes about the poor while challenging misperceptions about recipients of welfare programs such as Aid to Families with Dependent Children.[76] They ask Congress to continuously evaluate the minimum wage so that it corresponds with increasing inflation.[77] They support job training programs and affirmative action.[78] They recommend continuous evaluation of the tax system to ensure that sufficient taxes are raised "to pay for the public needs of society, especially to meet the basic needs of the poor."[79] They further insist that income tax rates be progressive and that families that fall below the poverty level should not be forced to pay income taxes.[80] In short, the U.S. Catholic Bishops would call not only for a continuation but an extension of the type of policies formulated through New Deal legislation.

Turning their attention to the transformation of America's food production from traditional family farms to agribusiness, the U.S. Catholic Bishops point out, "Today nearly half of U.S. food production comes from the 4 percent of farms with over $200,000 in gross sales." On the one hand, they admit that agribusiness is often more efficient and able to pass along lower food prices to the consumer. The problem with this transformation, according to the Catholic bishops, is that "This has led them to replace human labor with cheaper energy, expand farm size to employ new technologies favoring larger scale operations, neglect soil and water conservation, underpay farmworkers, and oppose farmworker unionization."[81] Moreover, higher concentrations of land in the hands of fewer people undermine the bishops' basic principles of bringing the working class closer to the propertied class and approximating a balance of power between laborers and those who own the means of production. In response to this crisis, they recommend that Congress provide emergency credit to family farmers and the rural lending institutions that have supported them, establish federal farm programs, and reform tax policies to benefit medium-sized family farms as opposed to large corporate farms.

After addressing the plight of America's poor, they turn to the relationship between the United States and the Third World. The National Conference of Catholic Bishops points out that U.S. policies tend to foster dependency rather than development.[82] Rather than improving the standard of living for citizens of the Third World, they would argue that "contracts" between parties of unequal power are largely responsible for the hunger, poverty, and infant mortality rates of the Third World. Rather than calling for a more radical transformation of the international economic order, however, the U.S. Catholic Bishops appeal to individual nations, multilateral institutions such as the United Nations, and transnational corporations to address these issues.[83]

Near the conclusion of *Economic Justice for All,* the National Conference of Catholic Bishops clarifies its contributions to the U.S. economic policy debates. "The United States prides itself on both its competitive sense of initiative and its spirit of teamwork. Today a greater spirit of partnership and teamwork is needed; competition alone will not do the job."[84] Though still identifying themselves with a moral center that lies between and beyond *laissez faire* capitalism and socialism, they seek to nudge a U.S. population slightly to the Left. They emphasize public responsibility, justice, and the common good in a nation that prefers to emphasize personal responsibility, freedom, and self-interest.

The principles articulated in *Economic Justice for All* continue to shape the resolutions adopted by the National Conference of Catholic Bishops on issues such as health care reform and welfare reform (as are discussed in Chapters 6 and 7 respectively). The influence of Catholic social teaching on U.S. Catholics and upon U.S. public policy is difficult to assess.

Catholic social teaching seems to have had some influence on lay Catholics. Public opinion polls consistently identify American Catholics as holding a moderate position on economic issues, including support for government activity, for welfare spending, and for U.S. government efforts to assist African Americans. Kenneth Wald points out that Roman Catholics stand Left of evangelical and Mainline Protestants but right of Jews and African Americans on all of these issues.[85] Although Catholics stand somewhat right of their own bishops on issues of economic justice, they are significantly more supportive of government programs to help the poor than non-Catholics with the same socioeconomic status. As in the case of American Jews, history and theology— not crass economic self-interest—best explain American Catholic support for government programs to help the poor. At the same time, however, Catholics wish to counter the lingering criticism that Catholics must not think for themselves but simply accept the teachings of their leaders without question.[86]

Meanwhile, the majority of American citizens seem to be moving in the direction opposed by the U.S. Catholic Bishops: rather than expanding welfare legislation, promoting greater opportunities for those on the margins of the economy, and emphasizing social justice, U.S. public opinion has marched steadily to the Right. How much further or more quickly this process would have taken place without the influence of the bishops is not easily measured. However, the assertion that the U.S. Catholic Bishops' 1983 pastoral letter on war and peace was far more influential than their 1986 pastoral letter on the economy is wholly convincing.[87] That the Catholic bishops' position on abortion has been more influential than their position on economic justice seems so obvious that it is hardly worth mentioning.

While the National Conference of Catholic Bishops has avoided purely partisan politics, the same cannot be said for individual bishops. While the term "culture wars" is best reserved for the conflict between evangelical and Mainline Protestant leaders who conceptualize politics as war by other means, the Catholic Church has also felt the pressure of the contemporary culture wars. As Timothy Byrnes points out, we can discern two camps within the National Conference of Catholic Bishops:

> The first camp is made up of bishops who emphasize a whole series of modern threats to human life. These bishops approach issues such as abortion, nuclear weapons, poverty, and capital punishment in a more or less even-handed way. They argue that paying too much attention to abortion unnecessarily narrows the church's prolife concerns and blunts the potential political effectiveness of what they call the consistent ethic of life or seamless garment of human dignity. . . . Opposed to this camp is a group of bishops who believe that abortion should be the American church's first political priority.[88]

Those who are willing to reduce Catholic social teaching to the single issue of abortion have often contributed to partisan politics that benefit the Republican Party.[89] There is no comparable contingent of bishops who have lifted up a single issue associated with the Left in order to help Democratic candidates. Those bishops who emphasize the consistent ethic of life, who recognize that no party perfectly reflects Catholic moral values, yet remain willing to be relevant in the real world of politics are the ones most capable of positively contributing to U.S. public policy debates.

No longer on the margins of U.S. society, the National Conference of Catholic Bishops is uniquely situated to mediate the culture wars, to find the common ground beyond the inflammatory rhetoric, and to foster the new vital center for U.S. public policy debates, that is, if they can avoid the temptation to reduce their social teachings to any single issue. Far from tragic or absurd, this new role is, nevertheless, ironic for a Catholic community that has perceived itself as an embattled minority for much of U.S. history.

NOTES

1. See Timothy A. Byrnes, *Catholic Bishops in American Politics* (Princeton: Princeton University Press, 1991), 3–34.

2. For a series of essays that provide powerful historical insights into the different ethnic groups that have immigrated to the United States, see Delores Liptak, ed., *A Church of Many Cultures: Selected Historical Essays on Ethnic American Catholicism* (New York: Garland Publishing, 1988).

3. For a more thorough analysis of anti-Catholic violence, see Ray Allen Billington, *The Protestant Crusade 1800–1860: A Study of the Origins of American Nativism* (New York: Rinehart, 1938). Donald L. Kinzer, *An Episode in Anti-Catholicism: The American Protective Association* (Seattle: University of Washington Press, 1964).

4. For a concise analysis of the Protestant nature of public education, see Vincent P. Lannie, "Alienation in America: The Immigrant Catholic and Public Education in Pre–Civil War America," *The Review of Politics* 32 (1970), 503–21.

5. Byrnes, *Catholic Bishops,* 17.

6. (Of course Africans who had involuntarily come to the United States as slaves suffered an even graver fate!) I am in the process of exploring the Irish Catholic heritage of my own family tree. My great-great-great-grandfather, Patrick Walsh, was one of these immigrants who settled in Ludlow, Illinois. (The name Walsh means *foreigner.* Originally, Walsh, Welsh, Welch, and Wallace all referred to someone from Wales. Over time, these names came to be applied to any stranger. Thus, I like to proclaim that a Walsh is a stranger from a strange land.)

7. For a deft analysis of poverty for Irish American Catholics, see Lawrence J. McCaffrey, *The Irish Diaspora in America* (Bloomington: Indiana University Press, 1976).

8. For a more detailed account of nineteenth-century Catholic reactions to labor unions, see R. Emmett Curran, "Confronting 'The Social Question': American Catholic Thought and the Socio-Economic Order in the Nineteenth Century," *U.S. Catholic Historian* 5 (1986), 165–94.

9. Henry J. Browne, *The Catholic Church and the Knights of Labor* (Washington, D.C.: University of America Press, 1949), 373. For a fuller account of Gibbons' influence, see John Tracy Ellis, *The Life of James Cardinal Gibbons: Archbishop of Baltimore, 1834–1921* (Milwaukee: Bruce, 1952).

10. In response to Protestant claims that the Catholic Church opposed civilization, democracy, and progress, Ireland argued that Catholicism was their true source. Looking around, however, he concluded that the Church was not appropriately fulfilling this function. Therefore, he sought to reform the American Church "on behalf of 'progress' and the temporal welfare of man." See Thomas E. Wangler, "John Ireland's Emergence as a Liberal Catholic and Americanist: 1875–1887," *Records of the American Catholic Historical Society* 81 (1970), 72. Pope Leo XIII would criticize certain elements of this view, the "Americanist" heresy. See Thomas McAvoy, *The Great Crisis in American Catholic History: 1895–1900,* (Chicago: H. Regnery Co., 1957).

11. Pope Leo XIII, *Rerum Novarum,* in *Proclaiming Justice & Peace: Papal Documents from Rerum Novarum through Centesimus Annus,* eds. Michael Walsh and Brian Davies (Mystic, Conn.: Twenty-Third Publications, Expanded, North American Edition, 1991), 17.

12. Walsh and Davies, eds. *Proclaiming Justice & Peace,* 32.

13. Ibid., 17.

14. Ibid., 18.

15. Ibid., 21.

16. Ibid., 22.

17. Ibid., 25. Liberation theologians and other Catholics who analyze poverty in terms of social systems would pick up this theme of a "preferential option for the

poor." See Donald Dorr, *Option for the Poor: A Hundred Years of Vatican Social Teaching* (Maryknoll, N.Y.: Orbis Books, 1983). Also see Gustavo Gutierrez, *A Theology of Liberation: History, Politics and Salvation,* ed. and trans. Caridad Inda and John Eagleson, (Maryknoll, N.Y.: Orbis Books, 1973).

18. Walsh and Davies, eds., *Proclaiming Justice & Peace,* 27.

19. Ibid., 28.

20. Ibid., 30. Such notions anticipate the principle of subsidiarity, the notion that power be exercised at the most individual or local level as possible but at the most regional or global level as necessary.

21. Ibid., 28.

22. Ibid., 30.

23. Ibid., 31.

24. Ibid., 33.

25. Ibid., 34.

26. Hugh J. Nolan, ed., *Pastoral Letters of the United States Catholic Bishops,* 4 vols. (Washington, D.C.: United States Catholic Conference, 1984), 1,269. Note the continuities between the pastoral letter and John A. Ryan's own, *A Living Wage* (New York: Macmillan, 1906). For a good account of Ryan's influence upon American Catholic social teaching, see Charles E. Curran, "John A. Ryan," in *American Catholic Social Ethics: Twentieth Century Approaches* (Notre Dame: University of Notre Dame Press, 1982), 26–91.

27. Nolan, ed., *Pastoral Letters,* I, 255–71.

28. Ibid., 268.

29. Ibid., 270.

30. Ibid., 268.

31. Ibid., 270–71.

32. Ibid., 366.

33. Ibid.

34. Ibid., 367.

35. Walsh and Davies, eds., *Proclaiming Justice and Peace,* 41.

36. Pius XI, *On Reconstructing the Social Order (Quadragesimo Anno),* trans. Francis Joseph Brown (Chicago: Outline Press, 1947), 61.

37. For a fuller understanding of Pope Pius XI's critiques of even the more moderate and evolutionary forces of socialism, see Pius XI, *On Reconstructing the Social Order,* 62–65.

38. Ibid., 58.

39. Ibid., 59.

40. Ibid.

41. Ibid., 33.

42. Nolan, ed., *Pastoral Letters,* 369.

43. Ibid., 369–70.

44. Ibid., 376.

45. Ibid.

46. Ibid., 379.

47. Ibid., 379–80.

48. Byrnes, *Catholic Bishops,* 28. Among the most important legislation would be the Agricultural Adjustment Act (1933), the National Labor Relations Act (1933), The Tennessee Valley Authority Act (1933), the National Labor Rela-

tions Act (1935), the Social Security Act (1935), and the Fair Labor Standards Act (1938).

49. For deeper insights into Catholic contributions to these public policy debates, see David J. O'Brien, *American Catholics and Social Reform: The New Deal Years* (New York: Oxford University Press, 1968). Also note Charles Curran, *American Catholic Social Ethics: Twentieth Century Approaches* (Notre Dame, Ind.: University of Notre Dame Press, 1982).

50. Robert Booth Fowler and Allen D. Hertzke, *Religion and Politics in America: Faith, Culture, and Strategic Choices* (Boulder: Westview, 1995), 88. Though most Catholics identified with the New Deal coalition of the Democratic Party, some of their strongest critics were also Catholic. For deeper insights into the conservative wing of the Catholic Church, see Patrick Allitt, *Catholic Intellectuals and Conservative Politics in America: 1950–1985* (Ithaca: Cornell University Press, 1993). Also note Charles J. Tull, *Father Coughlin and the New Deal* (New York: Syracuse University Press, 1965).

51. For a fuller exploration of the obstacles facing a Catholic presidential candidate, see Lawrence H. Fuchs, *John F. Kennedy and American Catholicism* (New York: Meredith, 1967).

52. See "Chapter II: The People of God," in *Vatican II's Constitution on the Church*, in *The Documents of Vatican II*, ed. Walter M. Abbott (New York: Guild, 1966), 32, 34.

53. Ibid., 34.

54. Ibid., 35.

55. Ibid.

56. This changing of emphasis may be seen in relation to the Protestant Reformation's slogan, "the priesthood of all believers," the worldwide democratic revolution that had increasingly located authority in the consent of the governed rather than the divine right of kings, and by the egalitarian spirit of the civil rights (and arguably women's rights) movements.

57. The mandate for placing more authority in the national conferences is seen most clearly in "The Decree on the Bishops' Pastoral Office in the Church." See Walter M. Abbott, ed., *The Documents of Vatican II* (New York: Guild, 1966), 424–26.

58. Ibid., 273–74.

59. Pope John XXIII issued *Mater et Magistra* in 1961 and *Pacem in Terris* in 1963. Pope John XXIII contributed to Catholic social teachings by focusing upon the relationships between the industrialized and developing nations, emphasizing a somewhat stronger role for government than his predecessors, and criticizing the arms race fueled by the Cold War. See Walsh and Davies, eds., *Proclaiming Justice and Peace*, 81–156.

60. Pope Paul VI issued *Populorum Progressio* in 1967, *Octagesimo Adveniens* in 1971, and *Evangelii Nuntiandi* in 1975. Pope Paul VI would present critical analyses of the relations between the First and Third Worlds, between development and liberation, and between economics and politics while simultaneously arguing that the gospel cannot be reduced to political and economic liberation. See Walsh and Davies, eds., *Proclaiming Justice and Peace*, 221–67, 284–322.

61. Pope John Paul II issued *Redemptor Hominis* in 1979, *Dives in Misericordia* in 1980, *Laborem Exercens* in 1981, *Sollicitudo Rei Socialis* in 1987, and *Centesimus Annus* in 1991. Despite his personal exposure to Soviet oppression, he attempted to draw a moral equivalence between communist ideology and *laisse faire*

ideology. He focused upon human rights, elaborated upon the dignity of human work, and criticized the notion of inevitable progress. For further insights into the economic thought of Pope John Paul II, see Kevin P. Doran, *Solidarity: A Synthesis of Personalism and Communalism in the Thought of Karol Wojtyla/ Pope John Paul II* (New York: Peter Lang, 1996). Also note essays by J. Bryan Hehir, Robert Benne, Dennis McCann, John Langan, and others in Oliver F. Williams and John W. Houck, ed., *The Making of An Economic Vision: John Paul II's* On Social Concern (Lanham: University Press of America, 1991). Further note W. King Mott, Jr., *The Third Way: Economic Justice According to John Paul II* (Lanham, Md.: University Press of America, 1998).

62. From 1966 to 1975, the National Conference of Catholic Bishops did issue the following resolutions: the "Pastoral Statement on Race Relations and Poverty" in 1966, the "Resolution on Antipoverty Legislation" in 1967, the "Statement on Farm Labor" in 1968, the "Resolution on Crusade against Poverty" in 1969, the "Statement on Welfare Reform Legislation" in 1970, the "Statement on the World Food Crisis" in 1974, the "Statement on Feeding the Hungry" in 1975, "The Economy: Human Dimensions" in 1975, and another "Resolution on Farm Labor" in 1975. (The relative silence of the American Catholic Church regarding economic issues was further influenced by the priorities of Francis Cardinal Spellman, who was the archbishop of New York from 1939–1967. Often referred to as the "American Pope," Cardinal Spellman emphasized the anticommunism in Catholic social teachings. See John Cooney, *The American Pope: The Life and Times of Francis Cardinal Spellman* (New York: Times Books, 1984).

63. For diverging analyses of this pastoral letter, see Thomas F. Gannon, ed., *The Catholic Challenge to the American Economy: Reflections on the U.S. Bishops' Pastoral Letter on Catholic Social Teaching and the U.S. Economy* (New York: Macmillan Publishing Company, 1987). Also note Charles R. Strain, ed., *Prophetic Visions and Economic Realities: Protestants, Jews and Catholics Confront the Bishops' Letter on the Economy* (Grand Rapids, Mich.: Eerdmans, 1989). For a libertarian response to this pastoral letter, see Michael Novak, *Freedom with Justice: Catholic Social Thought and Liberal Institutions* (San Francisco: Harper and Row, 1984). For a communitarian response to this pastoral letter, see P. Travis Kroeker, *Christian Ethics and Political Economy in North America: A Critical Analysis* (Montreal: McGill-Queens University Press, 1995), 91–121.

64. National Conference of Catholic Bishops, *Economic Justice for All: Pastoral Letter on Catholic Social Teaching and the U.S. Economy* (Washington, D.C.: United States Catholic Conference, 1986), vii.

65. Ibid., ix–xi.

66. Ibid., x.

67. Ibid., xii. Also see 65–67.

68. Ibid., 6. For a recent critical analysis of the globalization of capitalism, see Michael Budde, *The (Magic) Kingdom of God: Christianity and Global Culture Industries* (Boulder: Westview Press, 1997).

69. *Economic Justice for All*, 8.

70. Ibid., 8–10.

71. Ibid., 13.

72. Ibid., 69.

73. Ibid., 70.

74. Ibid., 83–92.

75. Ibid., 91.

76. Ibid., 95. The role of the Catholic Church in the public policy debates regarding welfare reform is discussed in greater detail in Chapter 6.

77. Ibid., 98.

78. Ibid.

79. Ibid., 99.

80. Ibid.

81. Ibid., 108.

82. Ibid., 122.

83. For an example of the more radical attempt to transform the global marketplace, see Eduardo Galeano, *Open Veins of Latin America: Five Centuries of the Pillage of a Continent,* trans. Cedric Belfrage (New York: Monthly Review Press, 1973).

84. *Economic Justice for All,* 145.

85. Kenneth D. Wald, "The Religious Dimension of American Political Behavior," in *Religion and Politics in the United States,* 3d ed. (Washington, D.C.: CQ Press, 1997), 180–82.

86. Echoing the sentiment of Bishop John Ireland who wrote one hundred years ago, "Let there be individual initiative, layman need not wait for priest, nor priest for bishop, nor bishop for pope." See John Ireland, *The Church and Modern Society* (New York: D. H. McBride, 1897), 72. Perhaps even John Ireland would be shocked by the results of a 1993 Gallup Poll indicating that only 7 percent of contemporary American Catholics seek their bishops' advice on public policy issues. See Thomas C. Fox, "U.S. Catholics Loyal, Choose Moral Terms," *National Catholic Reporter* 29 (October 8, 1993), 22–26.

87. See Byrnes, *Catholic Bishops,* 128–31; Wald, *Religion and Politics,* 276–81.

88. Byrnes, *Catholic Bishops,* 6.

89. For a fuller analysis of how Archbishop Joseph L. Bernardin's comments during the 1976 election led to the public perception that the Catholic Church was supporting the Republican candidate, see Byrnes, *Catholic Bishops,* 68–81. For insights into how Republican strategists sought to unite the Catholic bishops with the New Right in the 1980 election, see Byrnes, 82–91. For an analysis of how Bishops John O'Connor and Bernard Law influenced the 1984 presidential election, see Byrnes, 92–126. For a fuller theological explanation of the consistent ethic of life, see Thomas G. Fuechtmann, ed., *Consistent Ethic of Life: Joseph Cardinal Bernardin* (Kansas City, Mo.: Sheed & Ward, 1988).

4

Liberal Christians, Secular Conservatives, and the Influence of Non-Christian Religions

The identification of religion with the Right and secularization with the Left has become so prevalent in the contemporary United States that the New Christian Right has rather successfully cast the Republican G.O.P. as "God's Own Party."[1] Yet such a simplistic assumption is problematic, particularly with respect to political economy, if we identify the Right with *laissez faire* capitalism and the Left with communism. Many religious communities project a liberal[2] or even socialist[3] vision of society. On the other hand, secular Americans tend to hold libertarian views on economic and social policy. A simplistic identification of religion with the Right and secularization with the Left is less of an empirical reality than it is an ideological tool in the contemporary culture wars. By shaping debates about contemporary moral issues as a culture war between the religious Right and the secular Left, both sides increasingly marginalize the religious Left and the secular Right. In this sense, the religious Right and the secular Left both benefit from successfully portraying public policy debates as a culture war with themselves as the principal actors.

As a theologically conservative but fiscally liberal African American, Stephen Carter criticizes the culture wars thesis from a distinctive perspective:

The public rhetoric of religion, which from the time of the abolitionist movement through the era of the "social gospel" and well into the 1960s and early 1970s had largely been the property of liberalism, was all at once—and quite thunderously, too—the special province of people fighting for a cause that the left considered an affront [abortion]. Since the 1970s, liberals have been shedding religious rhetoric like a useless second skin, while conservatives have been turning it to one issue after another, so that by the time of the 1992 Republican convention, one had the eerie sense [not only] that the right was asserting ownership in God—but [that] the left had yielded its rights.[4]

In his analysis of public rhetoric, Stephen Carter focuses upon the extraordinary role that elite opinion shapers of our society (in the media, universities, and the courts) play in shaping and interpreting ethical debates. These elite opinion shapers, he argues, often emphasize the humanism of religious humanists while emphasizing the religion of religious conservatives. Many of these elite opinion shapers, he contends, do not tend to be neutral observers of the culture wars but secular conservatives who wish to disabuse people of their religious beliefs while otherwise preserving the status quo.

If we wish to fully understand the contemporary culture wars, we must examine the role of secularization theories. The older secularization theories (advanced by Feurbach, Freud, Marx, and Nietzsche) and the newer "elite secularization theories" (advanced by Richard John Neuhaus, William Bennett, and George Weigel) may appear to be as different as night and day, but they are in fact two sides of the same coin. Both portray an arguably cosmic battle between defenders of religion and secular elites.[5] Both are weapons for winning "culture wars," not purely social scientific tools for perceiving society more accurately.

SECULARIZATION THEORIES BY THE CRITICS OF RELIGION

To understand the modern critique of theology, one should begin by looking at the works of Ludwig Feurbach. Feurbach, a German philosopher who lived from 1804 to 1872, had a profound impact upon later intellectuals such as Marx, Nietzsche, and Freud.[6] He describes religion as a projection of all that is best in humanity:

The divine being is nothing else than the human being, or, rather the human nature purified, freed from the limits of the individual man, made objective—i.e., contemplated and revered as another, a distinct being.[7]

Thus, for Feurbach, the attempt to understand religion is none other than an attempt to understand human nature. Theology, on the other hand, is the human attempt to justify one's position, one's actions, or one's beliefs in light of religion.[8] According to Feurbach, the most immoral, unjust, infamous things are justified by appeals to theology.

For Feurbach, religion is a natural response to the sorrows and suffering of life, to the unfulfilled hopes of the human race, and to the unsatisfied needs of individuals and communities. Feurbach goes so far as to suggest, "The end of religion is the welfare, the salvation, the ultimate felicity of man; the relation of man to God is nothing else than his relation to his own spiritual good; God is the realized salvation of the soul, or the unlimited power of effecting the salvation, the bliss of man."[9] Feurbach is sympathetic to religion, where religion is understood as an unreflective projection of all that is best in oneself through service to the greater human community.

To understand how religion becomes translated into theology, Feurbach explains, one must understand the role of faith. According to Feurbach, faith is "essentially a spirit of partisanship."[10] Either one is on God's side or one is against God:

Faith is essentially intolerant; essentially, because with faith is always associated the illusion that its cause is the cause of God, its honour his honour. . . . Faith left to itself necessarily exalts itself above the laws of natural morality. The doctrine of faith is the doctrine of duty towards God. . . . By how much God is higher than man, by so much higher are duties to God than duties towards man.[11]

Thus, by identifying one's own will as the will of God, people are able to coerce others and justify themselves, even when they are clearly violating the natural standards of morality as in the case of inquisitions or holy wars. Feurbach contends that self-justification lies at the heart of theology.

At the end of his book, Feurbach summarizes his argument with the following thesis: "Man is the God of Christianity, Anthropology the mystery of Christian Theology." Identifying the significance of his work, he would proclaim:

[I]ts fundamental ideas, though not in the form in which they are here expressed, or in which they could be expressed under existing circumstances, will one day become the common property of mankind; for nothing is opposed to them in the present day but empty, powerless illusions and prejudices in contradiction with the true nature of man.[12]

Feurbach's theory of projection, his critique of blind faith, his emphasis upon the role of self-interest in the construction of theology, his affirmation of human dignity, and his commitment to enlightening the masses—these themes would influence other theorists who would shape the academic disciplines of modern psychology, sociology, and, to a lesser extent, philosophy.[13] Expanding upon Feurbach's thesis, the secularization theories of Marx, Freud, and Nietzsche paint a battle between the secular progressives and the religious reactionaries. They draw upon history to conclude that religion fosters violence, legitimates injustice, and hinders scientific advancement. That they might have found counterexamples in history, where appeals to religion seemed to promote peace or justice, seems irrelevant. Their point was not so much to describe the past but to shape a future in which human communities could evolve beyond the need for magic and superstition.

Drawing upon Feurbach's thesis, Marx articulated his most frequently cited critique of religion in 1844 where he describes religion as a drug that prevents the poor from promoting their truly vital interests:

The basis of irreligious criticism is this: *man makes religion,* religion does not make man. . . . *Religious* suffering is at the same time an *expression* of real suffering and a *protest* against real suffering. Religion is the sigh of the oppressed creature, the sentiment of a heartless world and the soul of soulless conditions. It is the *opium* of the people.[14]

Like a drug that helps people to tolerate the pain without removing the cause of the pain, Marx argues, the false promises of religious leaders, who are often little more than an extension of the ruling class, prevent poor people from expecting justice in this world. By proclaiming that those who toil and suffer in this world will find ultimate happiness in Heaven while those who demand justice in this world will go to Hell, Marx argues, religious leaders perpetuate a false consciousness that prevents the poor from promoting their truly vital interests. Therefore, Marx proclaims, the "abolition of religion as the *illusory* happiness of the people is the demand of their *real* happiness."[15]

Friedrich Nietzsche also argues that religion creates a false consciousness that prevents people from promoting their truly vital interests. He prophesies that a new breed of the human race is evolving beyond *homines religiosi,* religious men, and he anticipates, therefore, that society will progress. "All religions bear traces of the fact that they arose during the intellectual immaturity of the human race—before it had learned the obligations to speak the truth [1881]."[16] If "man" is unwilling to speak the truth, Nietzsche proclaims, the more highly evolved "Superman" is not.

Sigmund Freud, the father of modern psychology, claims that religion is like a childhood neurosis. In *The Future of an Illusion* (1927), Freud explains:

[R]eligion would be the universal obsessional neurosis of humanity. It, like the child's [neurosis], originated in the Oedipus complex, the relation to the father. According to this conception one might prophesy that the abandoning of religion must take place with the fateful inexorability of a process of growth, and that we are just now in the middle of this phase of development.[17]

Just as Freud believed that the process of maturation was essential for the development of a healthy individual, he argued that a similar process is necessary for human cultures.

Freed from illusion, Freud contends, human communities could adapt their laws and institutions as necessary to best satisfy the needs of the people:

[I]t would be an indubitable advantage to leave God out of the question altogether, and to admit honestly the purely human origin of all cultural laws and institutions.

Along with their pretensions to sanctity the rigid and immutable nature of these laws and regulations would also cease. Men would realize that these have been made, not so much to rule them, as, on the contrary, to serve their interests.[18]

By admitting the human construction of laws and institutions, human communities can adapt them, improve them, or discard them when they no longer serve the community.

Do these figures all share the same vision? At a superficial level, one might conclude that all forms of secularism converge. Nevertheless, the varieties of secularism are as potentially diverse as the varieties of religion. Figures who perceive religion as a problem to be overcome often draw this conclusion for the opposite—meaning incommensurate—reasons. Is religion problematic because rich people can appeal to theology to justify the oppression of the poor or because poor people can appeal to theology to prevent the advancement of the human race through a genuine meritocracy?

Karl Marx and Friedrich Nietzsche are both noted for a belief that religion is like a drug that prevents people from promoting their truly vital interests. Marx claims that religion drugs the poor into accepting injustice in this life with the false promise of a better life in the hereafter. If only the workers who must sell their labor in exchange for a wage could be purged of their religious beliefs, Marx concludes, they would demand justice, that is, an equality of control over the means of production. Nietzsche, on the other hand, claims that religion sentimentally encourages the strong to sympathize with the weak and thus to perpetuate, through charity, the survival of the least fit.[19] If only the strong could be purged of their religious beliefs, Nietzsche concludes, they would advance the human race through a genuine meritocracy. With respect to political economy, Karl Marx represents secularization of the Left, and Friedrich Nietzsche, secularization of the Right.

From their inception, theories of secularization have been politically charged. Jeffrey K. Hadden argues that the theory of secularization is "an orienting concept grounded in ideological preference rather than in systematic theory. Inertia, neglect, and an enduring ideological preference, rather than confirming evidence, have kept the theory more or less intact, at least until recently.[20] Hadden points to a lack of evidence to support the secularization theories as well as counterevidence, which, he contends, deals a serious blow to all secularization theories.

A news release by the Gallup organization emphasized the similarity of American attitudes toward religion in 1947 and 1997 (Table 4.1). The continuity of American attitudes upon such basic beliefs is hard to reconcile with the boldest of the secularization theories. While there have been some statistically significant changes—people are more tolerant of other religions, less likely to believe that God literally wrote their scriptures, and more likely to switch denominations—such social changes hardly amount to the end of religion.

Table 4.1
Americans' Attitudes toward Religion

1947	Attitudes	1997
95	% who claim to believe in God	96
73	% who claim to believe in an afterlife	71
90	% who claim to pray	90

Source: "Gallup: U.S. Religious Attitudes Similar to 1947," Religion News Service,
    14 May 1997.

Rodney Stark and William Bainbridge, who place the theory of secularization into a broader historical context, most astutely characterize the modern intellectual's "shock" about the breadth, if not the depth, of American religion:

At least since the Enlightenment, most Western intellectuals have anticipated the death of religion. . . . The most illustrious figures in sociology, anthropology, and psychology have unanimously expressed confidence that their children, or surely their grandchildren, would live to see the dawn of a new era in which, to paraphrase Freud, the infantile illusions of religion would be outgrown.[21]

While Stark and Bainbridge overstate the case,[22] they do point to the contours of this historical debate.

ELITE SECULARIZATION THEORIES BY THE DEFENDERS OF RELIGION

Members of the New Christian Right have responded to secularization theories with theories of their own. Richard John Neuhaus, William Bennett, and George Weigel articulate more academic versions of the "elite secularization" theories popularized by Rush Limbaugh, Pat Robertson, George Gilder, and others in recent years. They argue that it is not American society that is becoming progressively more secular but elites in norm-shaping institutions like education, the media, the Supreme Court, and even liberal churches.

Richard John Neuhaus, the most sophisticated proponent of the elite secularization thesis, uses the metaphor of the "naked public square" to describe how elites circumscribe faith-based moral arguments in the public realm:

The naked public square is the result of political doctrine and practice that would exclude religion and religiously grounded values from the conduct of public business. The doctrine is that America is a secular society. It finds dogmatic expression in the ideology of secularism. I will argue that the doctrine is demonstrably false and the dogma exceedingly dangerous.[23]

Hostile elites, he contends, control what America's children learn in school, what they see on television, and what laws rule the land.

Neuhaus, unlike the more radical Right, does not perceive a grand con-spiracy among these elites. Instead, he understands the contemporary cul-ture wars in light of the "disestablishment" of Mainline Protestantism. "We are witnessing today a contention between religious groups—evangelical, fundamentalist, Catholic—to succeed Mainline Protestantism as the culture-shaping force that provides moral legitimacy for democracy in America."[24] Neuhaus concludes that conservative religionists will increasingly influence American public policy and that the power of liberal elites in the Mainline Protestant churches will continue to erode.

Explaining why he thinks that the Mainline Protestant leaders are not only out of touch with their constituents but out of touch with reality as well, Neuhaus points to their stubborn adherence to outmoded views on political economy:

[Mainline Protestant leaders] persist in believing . . . that what happened in the 1980s and everything [since] is but a momentary interruption in the inexorable march toward liberalism's version of social justice. If we simply keep the faith and wait out the barbarians, the country will return to its senses and resume the uninterrupted march.[25]

Neuhaus argues that Mainline Protestant leaders have lost their credibility, not only among the larger public but also among their own constituents, in part, because of their liberal views on political economy.

Neuhaus paints Mainline Protestant leaders, along with other liberal elites, as the reactionaries trying to preserve the status quo of the New Deal era. In pointing out why the views of religious conservatives are more appropriate than the policies and programs of the New Deal era, Neuhaus proclaims, "Especially with regard to the poor, it is thought that such approaches did not do what they were supposed to do. The purpose, it should be remembered, was not to make it easier to be poor but to help the poor become no longer poor."[26] Rather than painting a picture of society marching inevitably toward greater secularization and liberalization, Neuhaus perceives secularization and liberalization as a cul-de-sac in human history, traveled by a small group of powerful elites.

Continuing his critique of the liberal elites who shape the social policy agenda of the Mainline Protestant churches, Neuhaus warns:

Leaders may strike a posture of prophetic protest for a time. They can and do rail against the political forces of darkness that have for a time, they believe, eclipsed the vision of Christian caring. But leaders who intend to remain in positions of believ-able leadership must after a while move toward their constituencies. Otherwise they will be viewed not as leaders but as leftovers, not as prophetic but as stubbornly wrongheaded.[27]

Because Neuhaus perceives secular and liberal elites to be "leftovers," he argues that religious conservatives are misguided to wage war against them.

"Religionists who rage against the 'secular humanist conspiracy' appear to be beating up on old people who might more kindly be left to their dreams of a brave new world that was not to be."[28]

Neuhaus, no less than Marx or Nietzsche, is appealing to a historical paradigm in an attempt to shape, not simply to describe, the course of history. His elite secularization theory is not a purely social scientific construct capable of clear empirical verification. It is a normative vision that identifies "true" religiosity with a conservative economic agenda and secularization with a liberal economic agenda.

SECULAR CONSERVATIVES

The assumption that secularization corresponds with liberal or socialist economic philosophies is, in part, due to a false conflation of secularization with Marxism. The notion that most people who drift from traditional religions embrace Leftist economic philosophies is demonstrably false. Most Americans who choose not to affiliate with religious communities tend to be rugged individualists, not communitarians. Their views are more likely to resonate with Social Darwinism than with Marxism. They are often consistent libertarians who advocate *laissez faire* policies when it comes to the legislation of morality and the redistribution of wealth. If they have increasingly left the Republican Party since the rise of the New Christian Right, it is because of their disdain for the New Christian Right's approach to social issues like abortion, homosexuality, and prayer in schools, not the Republican Party's economic policy proposals.

Focusing upon members of the U.S. Congress, Peter Benson and Dorothy Williams explored the relationship between religious values and public policy. Among the hypotheses that they tested were:

1. Political conservatives are more religious than political liberals.
2. Members of Congress who affirm basic Christian fundamentals adopt the politically conservative position of the New Christian Right: members who are atheists or secular humanists are politically liberal.
3. Members' religious beliefs and values bear little relationship to how they vote on specific issues, except for a few select areas like abortion and school prayer.[29]

They demonstrate that all three of these assumptions are false and identify them as myths about the influence of religion in politics.

Surveying the members of Congress, Benson and Williams noted that 80 percent claimed that religious convictions played more than a minor role in their political philosophies, party identification, and voting patterns.[30] The other 20 percent felt uncomfortable relating politics to religion: this constituency, far from being the most liberal, tended to be very conservative with respect to government spending, private ownership, and free enterprise.[31]

They tended to be rugged individualists who emphasize individual rights and personal responsibility, not social obligations and social responsibility.

The study by Benson and Williams might indirectly provide insights into the voting patterns of secular voters. Secular voters tend to be socially liberal but fiscally conservative. Because of their disdain for conservative social policies, secular voters have increasingly leaned toward the Democratic Party.[32] At the same time, secular voters have encouraged the Democratic Party to move away from its New Deal platform. A significant percentage of secular voters, moreover, seem to prefer a consistently libertarian candidate as reflected in their disproportionately high support for Ross Perot's presidential bid as an independent in 1992.[33]

Further challenging the notion that religion fosters conservative economic views while secular education fosters liberal economic views, a study by Timothy Clydesdale found the opposite to be more accurate. Analyzing the 1984 to 1996 General Social Surveys and the 1964 to 1990 National Election Data, Clydesdale comes to the surprising conclusion that "biblical conservatism intensifies expressions of concern for the poor" and "the experience of gaining a college degree appears to foster a status reinforcing perspective which rejects systemic solutions to poverty and accepts individualistic ones."[34] Before handing out Bibles and demanding lower budgets for state universities, liberals ought to explore this correlation in greater detail. While the study incorporates controls to counter the influence of age, race, and income, it does not distinguish between types of four-year degrees (technical or liberal arts), nor does it clarify whether the education causes people to be more conservative or whether the factors that encourage people to get an education also encourage them to view wealth and poverty in terms of individual initiative. In any event, Clydesdale identifies a positive correlation between higher education and conservative views on political economy and a negative correlation between theological conservatism and conservative views on political economy. Such findings challenge the ideological assumptions of cultural warriors on the Left and the Right.

LIBERAL CHRISTIANS

The first three chapters of this book challenge the simplistic assertion that religion in America has corresponded with *laissez faire* capitalism. Many theologians have played a significant role in justifying America's mixed economy by rejecting the extremes of Social Darwinism on the Right and Marxism on the Left. To varying degrees, Evangelicals, Mainline Protestants, and Roman Catholics have contributed to the New Deal Coalition that has shaped U.S. public policy for most of the twentieth century.

First, Evangelicals such as William Jennings Bryan, the three-time Democratic candidate for U.S. president, played a significant role in advancing the notion that people ought to be accountable for the well-being of each other and that government must play a role in fulfilling this function. Throughout much of the twentieth century, southern, white Evangelicals were important partners in the New Deal Coalition. In fact, Evangelicals were more likely to support government programs to assist the poor than non-Evangelicals. Increasingly, however, members of the New Christian Right have become the most vocal critics of the welfare state because they have been so busy avoiding Marxism that they have embraced Social Darwinism. They have been so busy challenging the concentration of power in big government that they have ignored the concentration of power in big business. Given that Evangelicals comprise over one-fourth of the U.S. population, the realignment of American Evangelicals will have a significant impact on the larger culture (see Chapter 1).

Second, the increasing identification of Mainline Protestants with the Democratic Party is among the most remarkable trends in religion and politics. Although they had been among the most ardent supporters of the Republican Party that opposed New Deal legislation, contemporary Mainline Protestants are almost evenly divided between support for Republican and Democratic candidates.[35] More significantly, Mainline Protestant leaders, perceiving themselves to be champions of peace and justice, tend to be much further Left than the U.S. population as a whole on issues such as welfare, affirmative action, health care reform, and campaign finance reform. Although the influence of Mainline Protestantism has diminished, this tradition still represents nearly one-fourth of the U.S. population (see Chapter 2).

Third, Roman Catholics have been among the most consistent contributors to the New Deal Coalition. Pronouncements by the U.S. Catholic Bishops and the Vatican, moreover, encourage their members to deepen their support for society's most vulnerable members through both private charity and government programs. The Catholic Church is likely to play a leading role in contributing to a new vital center for American public policy, not only because Catholics comprise one-fourth of the U.S. population, but because their leaders are often perceived by Evangelicals and Mainline Protestants as providing the greatest hope for mediating the contemporary culture wars (see Chapter 3).

AFRICAN AMERICAN CHURCHES IN THE NEW DEAL COALITION

African American Churches have also contributed substantially to the New Deal Coalition, but white Americans have generally dismissed their participation as merely a reflection of self-interest. Theology, they presume, is merely window dressing on the self-interested politics of the African American community (though they are far less likely to admit the role of self-interest in their own worldviews). By sociological standards, African Americans are among the most religiously orthodox and fiscally liberal people in the United States. A disproportionately high percentage of African

Americans claim to read their scriptures daily, attend religious services weekly, and believe that religion can solve most of society's problems.[36] Theologically, African Americans have more in common with conservative Evangelicals than they do with Catholics or Mainline Protestants; yet, since the time of the New Deal, African Americans have overwhelmingly identified with the Democratic Party. According to Fowler and Hertzke, "by the end of the 1960s the Democratic presidential nominee could count on receiving about 90 percent of the vote of the expanding black electorate."[37]

Nobody has done more to identify the Christianity of African Americans with social justice than Martin Luther King, Jr.[38] His dream of racial equality, rooted in the "brotherhood" of all people under one God, affirms the dignity of all people—regardless of their skin color, ethnicity, or class. While both sides in the contemporary culture wars claim to be heirs to his legacy, King clearly believed that government could play a constructive role in providing greater opportunities for society's most disadvantaged members. He was clearly not a Social Darwinist, a libertarian, or an advocate of *laissez faire* capitalism. In his last Sunday morning sermon, he warned:

Now there is another myth that still gets around; it is a kind of overreliance on the bootstrap philosophy. There are those who still feel that if the Negro is to rise out of poverty, if the Negro is to rise out of slum conditions, if he is to rise out of discrimination and segregation, he must do it all by himself. And so they say the Negro must lift himself by his own bootstraps. . . . but it is a cruel jest to say to a bootless man that he ought to lift himself by his own bootstraps.[39]

Martin Luther King, Jr., encouraged poor people to do what they could to help themselves, but he challenged more comfortable people to understand the systemic causes of poverty and to value the well-being of their "brothers and sisters." Moreover, he emphasized the role that government had played in helping Europe's peasants escape poverty through land grants, the role that government continues to play in protecting the property of the wealthy, and the role that government ought to play in helping America's poor.

Explaining why poor people cannot simply lift themselves up by the bootstraps, he elaborated upon the systemic nature of poverty:

When millions of people have been cheated for centuries, restitution is a costly process. Inferior education, poor housing, unemployment, inadequate health care— each is a bitter component of the oppression that has been our heritage. . . . Justice so long deferred has accumulated interest and its cost for the society will be substantial in financial as well as human terms. This fact has not been fully grasped, because most of the gains of the past decade were obtained at bargain prices.[40]

Elaborating upon the "bargain prices" of civil rights legislation, King pointed out that allowing blacks to sit next to whites on buses and in restaurants did not raise taxes. Providing disenfranchised African Americans with sufficient support so that they can become truly self-sufficient, he argued, will be a far more difficult task.

Anticipating that the working poor might face diminishing wages, King presented a powerful case that the new forms of automation in the mid-twentieth century have diminished the power of labor. Fewer people are needed to perform traditional tasks. As unemployment rises, the owners of the means of production can pit laborer against laborer to reduce wages and diminish the standard of living for the working class while simultaneously claiming higher profit rates for themselves. In response to these developments, King suggested, "Labor will have to intervene in the political life of the nation to chart a course which distributes to all instead of concentrating it among a few."[41]

In this last sermon, King would elaborate upon his Poor People's Campaign. In his interpretation of Luke 16:19–31, he explained that the rich man went to Hell, not because he was rich, but "because he sought to be a conscientious objector in the war against poverty."[42] King warned comfortable Americans:

I can hear the God of history saying, "That was not enough! But I was hungry and ye fed me not. I was naked and ye clothed me not. I was devoid of a decent sanitary house to live in, and ye provided no shelter for me. And consequently, you cannot enter the kingdom of greatness. If ye do it unto the least of these, my brethren, ye do it unto me."[43]

Appealing to a set of scriptures that serves as an embarrassment to Christian Social Darwinists, King spoke of the personal responsibility of the rich, not just the personal responsibility of the poor.

Elaborating upon the dangers of unbridled capitalism, Martin Luther King, Jr., described the life of the typical worker during the *laissez faire* capitalism of nineteenth-century America:

Less than a century ago the laborer had no rights, little or no respect, and led a life which was socially submerged and barren. He was hired and fired by economic despots whose power over him decreed his life or death. The children of workers had no childhood and no future. They, too, worked for pennies an hour and by the time they reached their teens they were wornout old men, devoid of spirit, devoid of hope and devoid of self-respect.[44]

King argued that the organized efforts by laborers raised the standard of living for most workers and increased, not decreased, American productivity.[45]

Familiar with the arguments of Nietzsche, King would argue that such justifications for the rich to get richer while the poor get poorer are antithetical to his understanding of Christianity:

Nietzsche's glorification of power—in his theory all life expressed the will to power—was an outgrowth of his contempt for ordinary morals. He attacked the whole of the Hebraic-Christian morality—with its virtues of piety and humility, its other-worldliness and its attitude toward suffering—as the glorification of weakness, as making virtues out of necessity and impotence. He looked to the development of a superman who would surpass man as man surpassed the ape.[46]

For King, Nietzsche's philosophy could not be reconciled with Christianity. Yet he felt that most libertarian arguments against compassion for the poor resonated with Nietzsche's themes.

Some of King's most vocal critics, while claiming to support economic justice and racial integration, criticized his appeals for *government* programs to help the poor. King would respond:

Now, people will say, "You can't legislate morals." Well, that may be true. Even though morality may not be legislated, behavior can be regulated. And this is very important. We need religion and education to change attitudes and to change the hearts of men. We need legislation and federal action to control behavior.[47]

To suggest that the solution to society's most vexing problems is *either* transforming hearts *or* controlling behavior, he contended, is a false dichotomy. He advocated both.

Although Martin Luther King, Jr., was clearly not a libertarian, it would be a mistake to identify him as a Marxist. His philosophy of nonviolent resistance undermined both philosophies. Influenced by the pacifism of Gandhi and Rauschenbusch, King rejected the Marxist principle that a season of violence can usher in a golden age. Influenced by the realism of Reinhold Niebuhr, King rejected the notion that human nature could be perfected if only we lived in a communist society. Looking into the history of Christian social ethics, he seemed to locate his own ethics as lying, in some sense, between the ethics of Walter Rauschenbusch and the ethics of Reinhold Niebuhr.[48]

When articulating his principle of nonviolent resistance, he would explain, "Christ furnished the spirit and motivation, while Gandhi furnished the method."[49] Thus, he would provide the following argument against any violent revolution to bring about justice:

To meet hate with retaliatory hate would do nothing but intensify the existence of evil in the universe. Hate begets hate; violence begets violence; toughness begets a greater toughness. We must meet the forces of hate with the power of love; we must meet physical force with soul force.[50]

King sought more than a Marxist vision of justice, he sought to make this world more like the Promised Land. Revolution by the oppressed, he argued, fails to comprehend the relationship between ends and means. He argued that for Christians, "The end is redemption and reconciliation. The aftermath of nonviolence is the creation of the beloved community, while the aftermath of violence is tragic bitterness."[51]

While identifying the libertarian movement with the rugged individualism that demonstrates no pity for the poor, King identified Marxism as a totalitarian collectivism that fails to appreciate the worth and dignity of the individual:

My reading of Marx also convinced me that truth is found neither in Marxism nor in traditional capitalism. Each represents a partial truth. Historically, capitalism failed to see the truth in collective enterprise and Marxism failed to see the truth in individual enterprise. Nineteenth-century capitalism failed to see that life is social and Marxism failed and still fails to see that life is individual and personal. The Kingdom of God is neither the thesis of individual enterprise nor the antithesis of collective enterprise, but a synthesis which reconciles the truths of both.[52]

Like other advocates of a mixed economy, he contended that the ideologies of *laissez faire* capitalism and communism represent the twin dangers of political economy.

JEWISH LIBERALISM

The Jewish community, though it represents less than 3 percent of the U.S. population, has been an important partner in the New Deal Coalition, in part, because Jews are "represented well beyond their numerical share of the population as candidates and officials, campaign activists, political contributors, members of interest groups, and—not least—as regular voters in primary and general elections."[53] After African Americans, Jews have most consistently affirmed the role of government in providing a safety net for the most vulnerable members of society. The simplistic assumption that economic self-interest explains theology becomes problematic when trying to understand the voting patterns of contemporary Jews. In the words of Fowler and Hertzke, "While they look like Episcopalians in economic status, they vote like blacks. Here we see the impact of a kind of value-based voting independent of social class."[54]

The Jewish community in America has long been identified with liberalism. While Franklin D. Roosevelt was president, the Central Conference of American Rabbis adopted the "Guiding Principles of Reform Judaism." Addressing the issue of social justice, they would conclude:

Judaism seeks the attainment of a just society by the application of its teachings to the economic order. . . . It aims at the elimination of man-made misery and suffering, of poverty and degradation, of tyranny and slavery, of social inequality and prejudice, of ill-will and strife. . . . It champions the cause of all who work and of their right to an adequate standard of living, as prior to the rights of property. . . . [It] strives for a social order which will protect men against the material disabilities of old age, sickness and unemployment.[55]

While the principles of the Columbus Platform do not identify any particular legislation, it is impractical to deny its continuities with the stated goals
of the New Deal programs being created at the time.

Lawrence Fuchs, among others, explains Jewish liberalism in terms of the
"Torah values" of learning, charity, and nonasceticism in relation to Jewish
history. Beginning with the central narrative of the Exodus (where God led
His people out of slavery in Egypt into the promised land), through the
Diaspora (when Jewish shtetls struggled to survive the pogroms by the dominant communities), to the Jewish ghettos in America, Jewish history proclaims that discrimination is real, that systemic injustices can foster poverty,
and that the world is not yet as God would like it to become. The notion
that God's judgment is based upon an individual's proclamation of faith
runs counter to most of Jewish history. For traditional Judaism, God's judgment is communal and takes place in this world. While some elements of
traditional Jewish theology have been forever transformed as a result of the
Holocaust, the notion that human beings are engaged in a covenant—that
human beings are accountable to and for each other—generally abides.[56]

Steven Cohen also elaborates upon the relationship between liberalism
and modern Judaism:

Many American Jews were raised with the understanding that liberalism or political radicalism constituted the very essence of Judaism, that all the rest—the rituals,
liturgy, communal organizations—were outdated, vestigial trappings for a religion
with a great moral and political message embodied in liberalism.[57]

Though Cohen is critical of Jews who would reduce Judaism to liberalism,
his argument, nonetheless, identifies this strong correlation in the self-
understanding of many modern Jews.

According to Cohen, Jewish liberalism has been most clearly demonstrated through support for the Democratic Party:

At least since the days of the New Deal, Jews, more than other Americans, have
been disproportionately "liberal," as inexact as the term might be. An extensive lit-
erature documents substantial Jewish support over the years for liberal, generally
Democratic Party candidates, even when they were opposed by politically moderate
Jewish Republicans.[58]

Jewish identity has been so linked to liberalism that a liberal (despite her
nominal religious affiliation) seems more "Jewish" than a conservative who
calls himself a Jew.

Explaining the correlation between Judaism and liberalism, Cohen argues
that modern Jews, who wished to integrate into American culture, could
further demonstrate their commitment to America by supporting policies
that contribute to the common good. "Certainly the generous social programs fostered by Democratic presidents, from Franklin Roosevelt to

Lyndon Johnson, drew upon several cultural elements and perspectives which were particularly attractive to Jews eager to participate in the larger society."[59] By extending their community of accountability to those outside the Jewish community, they encouraged non-Jews to reciprocate. By protecting the human rights of other vulnerable members of society, they hoped to preserve a respect for human rights that might also help their own community. Jewish liberalism, therefore, can be described as both a product of genuine altruism and enlightened self-interest.

Jewish organizations such as the Religious Action Center of Reform Judaism and the American Jewish Committee have appealed to ethics and to enlightened self-interest to justify their support for government programs to help the poor.[60] Yet few organizations have articulated the correlation between ethics, support for government programs to help the poor, and Jewish self-interest as explicitly as the National Jewish Community Relations Advisory Council:

These ethical concerns coincide with . . . protecting and fostering Jewish security. The social tensions and dislocations that are bred by want and inequality have erupted too often into threats and dangers to the democratic system in general, and the Jewish community in particular. For both of these reasons, issues of social justice have been, and remain, a priority concern of the Jewish community relations' field.[61]

While individual Jews might be "better off" if they do not help the poor and everyone else does, the council demonstrates that enlightened self-interest demands cooperation.

Such explanations might help to explain why support for social spending looms as the issue that most clearly distinguishes Jews from non-Jews. At the height of the Reagan revolution, a Gallup poll and a national survey of American Jews both asked, "Should the United States substantially cut spending on social welfare?" Fifty-six percent of American Jews responded, "No," compared to 28 percent of the American population.[62] Thus, the conclusion that [Reform] Judaism is only liberal with respect to social issues is misguided.

To conclude that the Jewish community is united in its support for the Democratic Party, however, is too simplistic. First, some Hasidic and Orthodox Jews have more in common with evangelical Protestants than with Reform Jews on issues such as abortion and voucher systems for private education. Second, tensions between African Americans and Jews since the 1960s have, at times, threatened to divide the New Deal Coalition. Third, the Republican Party has been a more ardent supporter of Israel than the Democratic Party in recent years (though the apocalyptic motives of some Christian fundamentalists create new problems for the Jewish community). Fourth, economic self-interest has prompted some Jews to reconsider their views on political economy. Fifth, some Jews, such as Milton Friedman and Irving Kristol, have been among the most prominent thinkers to articulate conservative views of political economy. Although most Jews continue to support a liberal economic agenda, they will continue to evaluate issues of economic justice in relation to other concerns. As long as the New Christian Right shapes the agenda of the Republican Party, however, there is little probability that Jewish voting patterns will change any time soon.

BEYOND CATHOLIC, PROTESTANT, JEW

In describing the religious landscape of 1955 America, the sociologist Will Herberg wrote:

The outstanding feature of the religious situation in America today is the pervasiveness of religious self-identification along the tripartite scheme of Protestant, Catholic, Jew. . . . Not to be—that is not to identify oneself and be identified as—either a Protestant, a Catholic, or a Jew is somehow not to be an American.[63]

Eighty-seven percent of all U.S. citizens still identify with these three categories, but many observers sense that the American religious landscape is being transformed by growing populations of Muslims, Hindus, and Buddhists, among others. None of these communities is currently well positioned to shape national politics. Moreover, the analysis of their current attitudes is limited because the sample for a typical national survey contains too few Buddhists or Hindus for reliable estimates about their views on issues such as health care reform and welfare reform. Nevertheless, these communities wield an increasing amount of influence, and they might also help us to explore the culture wars thesis.

Before testing the culture wars thesis on American Muslims, Hindus, and Buddhists, however, three social forces must be identified. First, Muslims who might be politically active in Iran, Buddhists who might be politically active in Japan, and Hindus who might be politically active in India will not necessarily be politically active upon immigrating to the United States. Religious minorities tend to demonstrate a sectarian attitude toward politics.[64] Perceiving the larger community as hostile, religious sects generally hope to be left alone. Second, most religious sects prefer to construct their own programs for redistributing wealth.[65] They neither expect to receive much support from the larger community, nor do they feel a sense of obligation for the well-being of the larger community. Therefore, one might identify this as a social source for religious minorities in the United States to prefer the economic policy proposals associated with the Republican Party. Third, immigrants are often the poorest, most vulnerable of all citizens. Therefore, one might identify this as a social source for recent immigrants and their families to prefer the economic policy proposals associated with the Democratic Party.

The culture wars thesis describes a cosmic battle between an ecumenism of orthodoxy that cuts across religious cleavages on one side and secular elites on the other. The ecumenism of orthodoxy consists of people who "order themselves, live by, and build upon the substance of a shared commitment to transcendent truths and the moral traditions that uphold them," while secular elites do not.[66] With respect to political economy, the orthodox are said to lean toward *laissez faire* capitalism while the apostates lean toward Marxism.

Islam

Based upon rates of birth, immigration, and emigration, the Muslim population in the United States will exceed the Jewish population by 2010.[67] Before assuming that this means that Muslims will be more influential than Jews, one must consider that Muslims are underrepresented in politics relative to their percentage of the population, that their relatively low economic standing further diminishes their political strength, and that they are often divided between orthodox and the Nation of Islam, Sunni and Shi'a, and between immigrant and indigenous. What unites the Muslim community in America is not a well-articulated philosophy on political economy but a common desire to challenge stereotypes about Muslims and a commitment to influence foreign policy, for example, by drawing attention to the plight of ethnic Albanians during the Kosovo Crisis, earthquake victims in Turkey, and most visibly, the Palestinians.[68]

This is not to imply that Muslims have no resources for addressing issues of political economy. As an orphan himself, Muhammad had consistently demanded that Muslims look after the orphans and the widows.[69] The Qur'an describes this duty to society's less fortunate members as an obligation owed to God.[70] Almsgiving to the poor is one of the Five Pillars of Islam.[71] Given that Muhammad was the political and spiritual leader at the time he wrote the Qur'an, moreover, there is no clear distinction between tithing and taxation. Therefore, one *might* conclude that government programs to assist the poor are perfectly consistent with Islamic social ethics.

Providing qualified support for this interpretation, the Islamic Council of Europe issued a resolution in 1976 that received a fair amount of attention. Given the heated conflicts between Muslims and Marxists during the Cold War, many Europeans were surprised that the council would describe the plight of "modern man" in terms that almost sounded Marxist: "He sees the powerful subjugating the weak, the rich dominating the poor, the 'have-nots' arrayed against the 'haves.' "[72] The council then went on to explain why Muslims support the principle of redistributing wealth:

Zakat commits man's wealth—his worldly resources—to the achievement of divine purposes in the socio-economic realm. *Zakat* is a monetary obligation. Every Muslim who possesses more than a certain minimum amount of wealth has to contribute at least a certain percentage of his total wealth for welfare functions of the society. It is not merely a charity; it is a religious right which the rich owe to the needy and poor, and to the society at large.[73]

Thus, the council clearly provides a theological justification for Muslims to contribute to the type of social welfare programs that are far more generous in Europe than in America. For some libertarians who had perceived Islam as an ally because of its historic hostility toward Marxism, this statement certainly came as a shock.

Yet, the Islamic Council of Europe does not speak for all Muslims in Europe, let alone all Muslims in America. The Islamic Society of North America might be able to provide that kind of political leadership, but it currently lacks solidarity; moreover, its leaders reject the kind of compromises necessary to become politically effective and fear that such active participation in American public life could lead to intolerable forms of assimilation. Such considerations led Steve Johnson, a scholar of Islam, to conclude, "No single organization appears capable of addressing the diversity of views about Islam and Islamic work among Muslims in America."[74]

While American Muslims have not raised a collective voice to articulate an economic policy position, it seems fair to claim that some Muslims would insist upon a radically different interpretation of the Islamic tradition than the more liberal view advanced by the Islamic Council of Europe. First of all, it is not clear to all American Muslims how giving money to Uncle Sam is the same as submission to God's will. Some Muslims might point to America's separation of mosque and state to conclude that religious communities, not the state, ought to meet the needs of society's orphans and widows. Finally, other Muslims might point to the notion of God's Providence, a central theme in the Qur'an, to explain that the world, as it currently exists, corresponds with God's will; therefore, the rich must be rich because God wants them to be rich and poverty is either a test or a punishment from God. In short, Muslims are likely to present a range of views on political economy not unlike the range found within Judaism or Christianity.

Political affiliation, moreover, is rarely based upon a single issue, particularly for a large community. On issues such as gender roles, abortion, and school vouchers, most American Muslims have far more in common with the New Christian Right than they do with liberal religionists.[75] On the other hand, Muslims are more likely to perceive the religious Left as their allies when it comes to fighting religious bigotry.[76] Given that their interests do not neatly coincide with either political party, moreover, it is difficult to anticipate how their views on political economy might be expressed in future public policy debates.

Buddhism, Hinduism, and Other Religions

After Islam, the two largest religious communities, Hinduism and Buddhism, each represent 0.5 percent of the U.S. population. The American public has demonstrated a fascination with figures such as Mohandas K. Gandhi and the Dalai Lama. Words like *karma* and *nirvana* have begun to creep into the vocabulary of all Americans. Yet most Americans have little understanding about how Hindu or Buddhist views on political economy might influence U.S. public policy.

When Americans think of Buddhism, they are far more likely to think of yoga than politics. If they do consider how Buddhism influences politics, they are likely to focus on issues of peace, ecological harmony, or the Most Favored Nation status of China. Buddhism, in the American mind at least, is associated with the renunciation of material wealth, not programs to redistribute wealth.

At the heart of Buddhism is the notion that the world, as ordinarily perceived, is empty, impermanent, and illusory. Nirvana corresponds with overcoming all dualisms to realize the *oneness* of all things. At one level, nirvana can seem like the ultimate goal—the singular desire that dispels all other temptations. Buddhists can withdraw from the world of illusions by joining a monastery, by climbing a mountain, or by finding some quiet place to meditate. Nothing seems further from enlightenment than the dirty world of politics. Yet some forms of Buddhism warn that the desire for personal enlightenment is among the greatest obstacles to the attainment of nirvana.[77] They also point out that those who truly understand the oneness of all things will act so as to relieve the suffering of others. In short, the range of Buddhist perspectives on politics is not unlike the range of perspectives found in the other world religions. The question, in part, is which forms of Buddhism might influence U.S. public policy. The type of Buddhism practiced by Hollywood's recent converts, for example, tends to be individualistic and largely apolitical.[78] Soka Gokkai International (SGI), on the other hand, is far more community focused and politically oriented. A recent issue of *SGI Quarterly*, for example, raised a number of critical questions about "the unregulated global casino" of international trade, warned that "the global economy is lurching out of control," and claimed that "the free market's so-called invisible hand is—and always was—our own."[79] Given their commitment to eliminating the suffering of others in this world, Soka Gokkai is more likely to play a small role in shaping American public policy than the sectarian forms of Buddhism.

While the obstacles that prevent Buddhism from influencing U.S. economic policy loom large, the obstacles are far greater for Hindus. Since most Americans equate Hindu economics with poverty and the caste system, Hindus who seek to influence public policy on economic issues will fight an uphill battle. A nuanced view of Indian history admits that some

Hindus have justified the suffering of the poor, but it also highlights the way that other Hindus have emphasized the ethical obligations that the rich owe to the poor.[80] Theistic Hindus advocate ethical perspectives that correspond with the range found in Judaism, Christianity, and Islam. Philosophical Hindus, who draw upon the teachings of the *Advaita Vedanta,* articulate ethical perspectives that resonate with the range of Buddhist perspectives. Among these various perspectives, which are truly Hindu and which represent apostasy? The conclusion that orthodox Hindus are those who advocate *laissez faire* capitalism seems to be more than a little bit biased.

CONCLUSION

Hinduism, like other world religions, says everything and nothing about political economy. That is, religions do not speak, think, or interpret; people do. World religions have been functional *and* dysfunctional, liberating *and* oppressive, true *and* false. World religions have survived, in part, because each contains a multitude of symbol systems capable of numerous interpretations. People whose views are shaped by a world religion must choose (or have chosen for them) which stories, doctrines, or paradigms will shape their understanding of a particular issue. Consider the following:

- Comfortable Hindus might appeal to the principles of karma, reincarnation, and moksha (enlightenment) as a justification for the status quo or as a source of ethical obligation.
- Oppressed people might appeal to the notion of God's Justice as a call to arms or as a source of hope.
- Comfortable Muslims might appeal to the concept of God's providence as a justification for the status quo or as a reminder of God's judgment.
- Jews might appeal to the notion of a covenantal relationship with God as a justification for ignoring the suffering of non-Jews or as an inspiration to honor the image of God in all people.
- Buddhists might point to the illusory nature of material wealth to conclude that the redistribution of nothing is nothing, or they might appeal to the illusory nature of material wealth to affirm that human dignity is far more valuable than video games and toaster ovens.
- Christians must choose which narratives (and which interpretations of those narratives) are going to shape their ethical obligations. When discussing a specific economic policy, it matters whether they emphasize the story about the tower of Babel or the story of the rich young ruler, the story of the man who misused his talents or the story of the prodigal son, Jesus' statement that there will always be poor people or his statement that whatever you do to the least of your brothers and sisters you do also to him.

- Secular Americans must also choose (or have chosen for them) which models will shape their conceptions of the cosmos and which narratives will shape their identities. When discussing a specific economic policy, it matters whether they conceptualize human beings as a conglomeration of atoms not qualitatively distinct from their own excrements or as creatures of inestimable worth.

At one level, the questions facing Catholic, Protestant, and Jew; Muslim, Hindu, and Buddhist; religionist, nominalist, and secularist are the same. The culture wars thesis demonstrates persuasively that the divisions within each tradition can be more politically significant than the divisions between traditions. The culture wars thesis, however, becomes problematic when its proponents paint a nearly cosmic battle between religionists who, among other things, support *laissez faire* capitalism and secularists who, among other things, affirm Marxist or liberal views of political economy.

The real battle in the United States as America begins to dismantle its welfare state is not between Marxist atheists (who represent less than one percent of the U.S. population) and all religious people. Americans on both sides of these public policy debates tend to be people whose views on religion tend to relate to their views on political economy in far more complex ways. Historically speaking, the implication that secular elites had imposed a Marxist welfare state upon an unsuspecting U.S. population is inaccurate. This view ignores the role of religious communities in providing theological arguments for the type of New Deal legislation that has shaped much of the twentieth century. Furthermore, the claim that all orthodox religionists affirm *laissez faire* capitalism is not supported by cross-cultural analysis. My emphasis upon religious liberals and secular conservatives is not a strategy for proclaiming that religious people are the "true progressives" so much as it is an attempt to balance the contemporary scholarship about how religion has influenced, and continues to influence, Americans' views on political economy.

NOTES

1. James L. Guth and John C. Green, "God's Own Party: Evangelicals and Republicans in the '92 Election," *Christian Century* 110, no. 5 (17 February, 1993), 172.

2. Here I am appealing to the definition of economic liberalism as a pragmatic orientation that seeks to ameliorate the tensions between personal and social responsibility, between liberty and justice, between Marxist and bourgeois ideologies. Economic liberalism has been most clearly exemplified in the United States through New Deal legislation that emphasizes social responsibility for promoting greater justice by regulating big business, using income taxes to moderately redistribute wealth, and otherwise reforming a fundamentally capitalist structure. Liberals reject both the socialist proposal to replace the free market with a planned economy and the libertarian proposal to simply let the free market run its course.

3. For insights into a religious movement that explicitly draws upon Marxist analysis as a source for theological reflection and biblical interpretation, see José Miranda, *Marx and the Bible: A Critique of the Philosophy of Oppression,* trans. John Eagleson (Maryknoll, N.Y.: Orbis Books, 1974).

4. Stephen Carter, *The Culture of Disbelief: How American Law and Politics Trivialize Religious Devotion* (New York: Anchor, 1994; reprint, New York: Basic Books, 1993), 58.

5. Nietzsche speaks of the Superman. Marx refers to the dictatorship of the Proletariat. Both envisioned elites playing a significant role in accelerating the process of secularization. Despite very different political agendas, they both appealed to elites to transform the ignorant masses and to replace superstition with truth.

6. For an understanding of how Marx, Nietzsche, and Freud, among others, draw upon Feurbach's thesis, see Van Harvey, *Feurbach and the Interpretation of Religion,* Cambridge Studies in Religion and Critical Thought I (Cambridge: Cambridge University Press, 1995).

7. Ludwig Feurbach, *The Essence of Christianity,* trans. George Eliot (New York: Harper & Row, 1957), 14.

8. Ibid., 213. That Feurbach's thesis would also serve as an inspiration to Karl Barth, author of *Church Dogmatics,* might shock many people, unless they realize that Barth thought Feurbach's critiques were far more relevant to liberal theology than to conservative theology. See Barth's "Introductory Essay" in Feurbach, x–xxxii.

9. Ibid., 185.

10. Ibid., 255.

11. Ibid., 255, 260.

12. Ibid., xliii.

13. In explaining why Feurbach is not "ranked among the masters of suspicion," Van Harvey explains, "Feuerbach's view that religion is a function of the emergence of self-consciousness leads to a far more complex interpretation of religion than that practiced by the other three masters of suspicion. . . . Indeed, it raises the fundamental question whether it is possible to make a sharp dichotomy between the hermeneutics of suspicion and the hermeneutics of charity." Harvey, *Feurbach and the Interpretation of Religion,* 13.

14. Karl Marx, "Contribution to the Critique of Hegel's Philosophy of Right," in *The Marx-Engels Reader,* 2d ed., ed. Robert C. Tucker (New York: W. W. Norton, 1978, 1972), 53–54.

15. Ibid., 54. Also note, Karl Marx and Friedrich Engels, *Karl Marx and Friedrich Engels on Religion* (New York: Schocken Books, 1964).

16. Friedrich Nietzsche, "Dawn: Thoughts on the Prejudices of Morality," in *The Portable Nietzsche,* ed. Walter Kaufmann (New York: Modern Library, 1992), Aphorism 91.

17. Sigmund Freud, *The Future of an Illusion,* trans. W. D. Robson-Scott (New York: Liveright Publishing, 1953), 78.

18. Ibid., 73.

19. Note the discussion of Nietzsche's philosophy in Chapter 1. Also note his summary of "The Religious Nature," in Friedrich Nietzsche, *Beyond Good and Evil: Prelude to a Philosophy of the Future,* trans. R. J. Hollingdale (New York: Penguin Books, 1990; reprint, 1973), 87–89. For a more in-depth exploration of how Nietzsche believes that Christianity has become a sentimental religion that identifies

with the weak while preventing the possibility of a genuine meritocracy, see Friedrich Nietzsche, "The Anti-Christ," in *The Portable Nietzsche,* trans. and ed. Walter Kaufmann (New York: Penguin Books, 1954).

20. Jeffrey K. Hadden and Anson Shupe, eds, *Religion and the Political Order,* vol. 3, *Secularization and Fundamentalism Reconsidered* (New York: Paragon, 1989), xvi. For an intelligent discussion of secularization theories from a variety of perspectives, see Phillip E. Hammond, ed., *The Sacred in a Secular Age: Toward Revision in the Scientific Study of Religion* (Berkeley: University of California Press, 1985).

21. Rodney Stark and William S. Bainbridge, *The Future of Religion* (Berkeley: University of California Press, 1985), 1.

22. Over the past 40 years, social scientists have increasingly embraced less reductionist models for interpreting religious beliefs, practices, and institutions than the discipline-shaping figures of Sigmund Freud, Karl Marx, and Bronislaw Malinowski. Horace Miner has provided the classic parody of social scientists who deny the possibility of their own ethnocentrism while interpreting the "other." See his "Body Ritual among the Nacirema," *The American Anthropologist* 58 (1956), 503–6.

23. Richard John Neuhaus, *The Naked Public Square: Religion and Democracy in America* (Grand Rapids: Eerdmans, 1984), vii.

24. Ibid.

25. Ibid., 41.

26. Ibid.

27. Ibid., 42.

28. Ibid., 24.

29. Peter Benson and Dorothy Williams, *Religion on Capitol Hill: Myths and Realities* (New York: Oxford University Press), 3. This study was performed in 1980, the dawn of the contemporary culture wars. In their methodology, they explain that they used personal interviews to devise the following typology: legalistic religionists, self-concerned religionists, integrated religionists, people-concerned religionists, nontraditional religionists, and nominal religionists (see 123–39).

30. Ibid., 143. In response to the question of whether religious beliefs influence their voting, Benson and Williams point out, "Political liberals are as likely to say 'moderate' or 'major' as are conservatives; Republicans are as likely as Democrats" (143). They conclude that liberals and conservatives "do not substantially differ in how often they go to church or read Scripture, or in their degree of commitment to religion or religious institutions. . . . The most accurate conclusion is this: *liberals and conservatives differ not in amount of religion, but in kind.* Overall, the conservative tends to adopt an Individualism-Preserving religion and the liberal tends toward Community-Building religion" (164).

31. Ibid., 161.

32. See Robert Booth Fowler and Allan D. Hertzke, *Religion and Politics in America: Faith, Culture, and Strategic Choices* (Boulder, Colo.: Westview Press, 1995), 104–5.

33. John Green, "Religion, Social Issues, and the Christian Right," in *Disciples and Democracy: Religious Conservatives and the Future of American Politics,* ed. Michael Cromartie (Grand Rapids: Eerdmans, 1994), 33.

34. Timothy T. Clydesdale, "Toward Understanding the Role of Bible Beliefs and Higher Education in American Attitudes toward Eradicating Poverty, 1964–1996," *The Journal for the Scientific Study of Religion* 38 (March 1999), 103. He also cites

evidence of similar conclusions by Stephen Hart, *What Does the Lord Require? How American Christians Think about Economic Justice* (New York: Oxford University Press, 1992); Robert Wuthnow, *God and Mammon in America* (New York: Free Press, 1994); James R. Kluegel and Eliot R. Smith, *Beliefs about Inequality: Americans' Views of What Is and What Ought to Be,* (New York: Aldine De Gruyter), 1986.

35. Jeff Manza and Clem Brooks, "The Religious Factor in U.S. Presidential Elections," *American Journal of Sociology* 103, no. 1 (July 1997), 38.

36. Cardell K. Jacobson, Tim B. Heaton, and Rutledge M. Dennis, "Black-White Differences in Religiosity: Item Analysis and a Formal Structural Test," *Sociological Analysis* 51 (1990), 257–70.

37. See Fowler and Hertzke, *Religion and Politics,* 157.

38. This is not to minimize the influence of more contemporary figures such as Jesse Jackson, T. J. Jamison, Joan Brown Campbell, Cornel West, or Andrew Young. For further insights into African American Christianity, see Peter J. Paris, *The Social Teaching of the Black Churches* (Philadelphia: Fortress Press, 1985).

39. Martin Luther King, Jr., "Remaining Awake through a Great Revolution," *Congressional Record* 114, no. 7 (9 April 1968), 9395–96.

40. Martin Luther King, Jr., "A Testament of Hope," *Playboy* 16 (January 1969), 194. In this article, he also states, "The Great Society has become a victim of the [Vietnam] war," 236.

41. Martin Luther King, Jr., "If the Negro Wins, Labor Wins," *Hotel* 10 (12 February 1962), 4. While pointing to the interconnected fate of labor and African Americans, King also challenges the persistence of discrimination in many labor unions.

42. King, "Remaining Awake," 9396.

43. Ibid.

44. King, "If the Negro Wins, Labor Wins," *Hotel* 10, 4.

45. Ibid., 202.

46. Martin Luther King, Jr., *Stride toward Freedom: The Montgomery Story* (New York: Harper & Row, 1958), 96.

47. Martin Luther King, Jr., "The American Dream," *Negro History Bulletin* 31 (May 1968), 14. For more specific insights into what King thinks is necessary for African Americans to become self-sufficient, see Martin Luther King, Jr., *Where Do We Go from Here: Chaos or Community* (New York: Harper & Row, 1967), 4–12, 193–202.

48. Ibid. Also note Howard Thurman's work that inspired King to explore Gandhi's philosophy of nonviolent resistance, *With Head and Heart: The Autobiography of Howard Thurman* (New York: Harcourt Brace Jovanovich, 1979), 103–36. Also note Mohandas K. Gandhi, *An Autobiography: The Story of My Experiments with Truth* (Boston: Beacon Press, 1957). For deeper insights into the Social Gospel of Walter Rauschenbusch, see *A Theology for the Social Gospel* (New York: Macmillan, 1917).

49. King, *Stride toward Freedom,* 85.

50. Ibid., 87.

51. Ibid., 102. For further insights into his critiques of communism, see Martin Luther King, Jr., "An Address before the National Press Club," *Congressional Record* 108 (20 July 1962), 14247–49.

52. King, *Stride toward Freedom,* 95.

53. Kenneth D. Wald, *Religion and Politics in the United States*, 3d ed., (Washington, D.C.: CQ Press, 1997), 310.

54. Fowler and Hertzke, *Religion and Politics*, 105. In making this statement, they concede that this characterization is "a slight exaggeration." For further insights into the common ground between Jews and African Americans and why they support similar economic policy proposals, see Lynn F. Landsberg and David Saperstein, eds., *Common Road to Justice: A Programming Manual for Blacks and Jews* (Washington, D.C.: Religious Action Center of Reform Judaism, 1991), 9–16.

55. Central Conference of American Rabbis, "Guiding Principles of Reform Judaism (1937)," in Michael A. Meyer, *Response to Modernity: A History of the Reform Movement in Judaism* (New York: Oxford University Press, 1988), 388–94. For further insights into the role of Benjamin V. Cohen, Abe Fortas, Myer Feldman, and other Jewish presidential aids who helped to draft legislation from the "New Deal" to the "Great Society," see Stephen D. Isaacs, *Jews and American Politics* (New York: Doubleday & Co., 1974).

56. Lawrence Fuchs, *The Political Behavior of American Jews* (Glencoe, Ill.: Free Press, 1956), 171–203. For a deeply personal account of how the ethics of Judaism can inspire a liberal democratic philosophy, see Neal Riemer, "Judaism: A Living Option for Modern Man," *Jewish Heritage* (Fall 1961), 42–47. Also note Meir Tamari, *With All Your Possessions: Jewish Ethics and Economic Life* (New York: Free Press, 1987), 242–77.

57. Steven M. Cohen, *American Modernity and Jewish Identity* (New York: Travistock, 1983), 35.

58. Ibid., 134. Neal Riemer points out, "The average Jewish percentage vote for the Democratic presidential candidate from 1928 to 1988 was 75 percent." See Neal Riemer, "Jewish Voting Patterns in Previous Presidential Elections," *Metro West: Jewish News* (29 October 1992), 15. In 1992 78 percent of all Jews voted for Clinton, 12 percent for Bush, and 10 percent for Perot. See Neal Riemer, "Jewish Voting Patterns in the Election," *Metro West: Jewish News* (19 November 1992), 44.

59. Ibid., 35.

60. For further insights into the American Jewish Committee's critique of communism and corresponding defense of liberalism, see Naomi W. Cohen, "Between Left and Right," in *The American Jewish Committee: 1906–1966* (Philadelphia: Jewish Publication Society of America, 1972), 345–82.

61. National Jewish Community Relations Advisory Council, *Joint Program Plan* (New York, 1983–1984), 37.

62. Ibid. 140.

63. Will Herberg, *Protestant, Catholic, Jew: An Essay in American Religious Sociology* (Garden City, N.Y.: Doubleday, 1955), 272, 274.

64. Inspired by Ernst Troeltsch's classic distinction between church, sect, denomination, and cult, H. Richard Niebuhr explored how a religious community relates to the larger culture. Though his terms and examples are overly Christian, I would contend that the underlying sociological theory is more generally applicable for understanding island cultures in a nation like the United States. See H. Richard Niebuhr, *Christ and Culture* (New York: Harper & Row, 1951; reprint 1956), 29–82.

65. The Amish, Hasidic Jews, the Nation of Islam, and the Church of Jesus Christ of Latter Day Saints, among others, tend to create internal systems for redistributing wealth. The Mormon welfare system has often been lifted up as a model of religious giving. See Garth Mangum and Bruce Blumell, *The Mormon's War on Poverty: A History of LDS Welfare, 1830–1990* (Salt Lake City: University of Utah Press, 1993). It will be interesting to see if Mormons will continue the high commitment to their members as their community is in the process of shifting from a sectarian stance to American culture to a more mainstream denomination. See Jan Shipps, "Mormon Metamorphosis: The Neglected Story," *The Christian Century* 113, no. 24 (14 August 1996), 784–87.

66. James Davison Hunter, *Culture Wars: The Struggle to Define America* (New York: Basic Books, 1991), 126, 329 (footnote 16).

67. Mary Dejevsky, *The Plain Dealer* (26 March 1998), 11B. To understand the magnitude of this shift, it might be helpful to note that the United States had only one mosque and less than 20,000 Muslims in 1934.

68. The Council on American-Islamic Relations (CAIR), for example, has not wanted to draw attention away from its central mission of challenging Islamophobia by adopting controversial proposals on issues such as health care reform or welfare reform. Their web site is http://www.cair.com.

69. For deeper insights into the life of Muhammad, see Ghulam Malik, *Muhammad: an Islamic Perspective* (Lanham, Md.: University Press of America, 1996).

70. For example, see the Qur'an 2:177, 3:180, 4:1–2, 8:41.

71. For further insights into the development of the *Sharia,* Islamic law, see John L. Esposito, *Islam: The Straight Path* (New York: Oxford University Press, 1988).

72. "Statement by the Islamic Council of Europe" (London: Islamic Council of Europe, 1976), 1. While contemporary Muslims have sometimes identified the partial truth of Marxist critiques of capitalism, they have also identified the partial truths of capitalist critiques of communism. Perhaps this helps to explain the animosity toward both the East and the West during the Cold War by many nations with a Muslim majority.

73. Ibid., 3. For an elaboration upon Islamic views on taxation, see Azim A. Nanji, "Ethics and Taxation: The Perspective of the Islamic Tradition," *The Journal of Religious Ethics* 13.1 (Spring 1985), 166–177. In describing the views of contemporary Muslim writers, Nanji concludes that they avoid "both a system of unfettered capitalism and of communism with its policy of outright state ownership of resources. If some framework of private enterprise and ownership is maintained by most Muslim countries, then concern for a tax policy incorporating Islamic values becomes very pertinent" (174).

74. Steve A. Johnson, "Political Activity of Muslims in America," in *The Muslims of America,* ed. Yvonne Yazbeck Haddad (New York: Oxford University Press, 1991), 122.

75. See Fowler and Hertzke, *Religion and Politics,* 191.

76. Byron L. Haines, "Perspectives of American Churches on Islam and the Muslim Community in America: An Analysis of Some Official and Unofficial Statements," in *The Muslims of America,* ed. Yvonne Yazbeck Haddad (New York: Oxford University Press, 1991), 39–52.

77. For a discussion of this view that enlightenment fosters compassion, see Clarence H. Hamilton, *Buddhism: A Religion of Infinite Compassion* (New York:

Liberal Arts Press, 1954; reprint 1952). For a more nuanced analysis of the relationship between Buddhist ethics and political economy, see Phra Rajavaramuni, "Foundations of Buddhist Social Ethics," in *Ethics, Wealth and Salvation,* eds. Russell F. Sizemore and Donald K. Swearer (Columbia: University of South Carolina Press, 1990), 29–53.

78. For a discussion of Buddhism in America, particularly as it relates to Hollywood, see "Buddhism in America," *Time* 150, no. 15 (13 October 1997). For a good collection of essays describing the various forms of Buddhism in America, see Charles S. Prebish and Kenneth K. Tanaka, eds., *The Faces of Buddhism in America* (Berkeley: University of California Press, 1998).

79. Hazel Henderson, "The Love Economy: Toward Sustainable Human Development," *SGI Quarterly: Buddhist Perspectives on Peace, Culture and Education* (October 1998), 3–7. One of my students, Brian Johnson, wrote an unpublished paper that identifies certain parallels between Soka Gakkai and the Social Gospel Movement of liberal Protestantism. For a more critical analysis of the Soka Gakkai movement in Japan, see Anson Shupe, "Militancy and Accommodation in the Third Civilization: The Case of Japan's Soka Gakkai Movement," in *Prophetic Religions and Politics,* eds. Jeffrey K. Hadden and Anson Shupe (New York: Paragon House, 1986), 235–53.

80. Ananda Coomaraswamy, "What Has India Contributed to Human Welfare," in *The Dance of Shiva* (New York: Dover Publication, 1985; New York: Sunwise Turn, 1924), 2–17. For a broad overview of the relationships between religion and economics in India, Iran, Mexico, Japan, and Nigeria, see James Finn, ed., *Global Economics and Religion* (New Brunswick: Transaction Books, 1983).

Part II

Economic Policy Debates
of the 1990s

5

Health Care Reform

Mainline Protestant churches, the Catholic Church, and America's Jewish communities have been criticizing the American health care system for much of the New Deal era. They contend that access to health care ought to be understood as a basic human right. They point out that the United States is the only industrialized nation that does not guarantee access to primary and preventive health care for all its citizens. Organizations like the Christian Coalition, on the other hand, clearly opposed any attempt to expand the power of the federal government and to redistribute more wealth from America's more comfortable citizens to pay for the health care of poor people.

THE ROMAN CATHOLIC CHURCH

On November 19, 1981, the National Conference of Catholic Bishops (NCCB) issued its most comprehensive statement on health care reform to date. This resolution, "Health and Health Care," offered "some basic principles for public policy."[1] In cooperation with the Catholic Health Association, Catholic Charities, and the United States Catholic Conference,[2] the NCCB stated, "Every person has a basic right to adequate health care. This right flows from the sanctity of human life and the dignity that belongs to all human persons, who are made in the image of God. It implies that access to that health care which is necessary and suitable for the proper development and maintenance of life must be provided for all people, regardless of economic, social, or legal status. Special attention should be given to meeting the basic health needs of the poor."[3]

The NCCB elaborated upon its national health care policy recommendations by insisting, "In any national health system, provision should be made for the protection of conscience in the delivery of care. This applies not only to individual and institutional providers, but also to consumers."[4] In other words, the NCCB opposed any policy that would require health care providers to perform (or patients to receive) abortions, euthanasia, or other procedures deemed immoral by the Catholic Church.

In contrast to the current laws in the United States that guarantee only catastrophic health care, the NCCB proposes, "The benefits provided in a national health care policy should be sufficient to maintain and promote good health as well as to treat disease and disability. . . . [P]ublic policy should provide incentives for preventive care, early intervention, and alternative delivery systems."[5] While calling for an expansion of federally guaranteed health care to include primary and preventive services, they simultaneously criticize any proposal for a nationalized medical plan that would eliminate administrative control by independent health care providers or deny consumers any legitimate choice of providers.

Given the administrative quagmire of our current health care anarchy, the NCCB claims, "Public policy should ensure that uniform standards are part of the health care delivery system."[6] Not only is this necessary to ensure that the poorest citizens will receive adequate health care, but such standards can eliminate some of the paperwork, preauthorization calls, and other administrative costs that do not directly improve the quality of health care for the patient.

Summarizing the central point of their message, the NCCB proclaims, "Following on the principles and on our belief in *health care as a basic human right,* we call for the development of a national health insurance program. It is the responsibility of the federal government to establish a comprehensive health care system that will ensure a basic level of health care for all Americans. *The federal government should also ensure adequate funding for this basic level of care through a national health insurance program*" [emphasis added].[7] Though their proposal does not specify how this funding is to be obtained (through income taxes, employer mandates, or some other means), it clearly holds the federal government responsible for ensuring that this right to health care is fulfilled.

MAINLINE PROTESTANT DENOMINATIONS

Many denominations associated with Mainline Protestantism (such as the Episcopal Church, the United Methodist Church, and the Presbyterian Church U.S.A.) have adopted resolutions calling for health care reform in the United States. Rather than outlining the resolutions issued by each denomination, I will focus on the resolutions adopted by the Presbyterian Church. The Presbyterian Church has supported a national policy of universal access to high quality health care since 1946. Two of their more recent resolutions, however, were particularly detailed and relevant to the public policy debates surrounding health care reform in 1994. In 1988, the general assembly of the Presbyterian Church adopted a policy statement entitled *Life Abundant: Values, Choices, and Health Care*. Some of the more powerful statements in this document identify universal access to health care as a human rights issue, not merely a commodity to be consumed by society's more comfortable members:

Society and its constituent public, private, and voluntary organizations have a duty—a moral obligation—to promote a healthful environment and to assure the availability of health-giving resources to all people. Free markets alone cannot provide for the adequate supply and equitable distribution of these resources.[8]

If the free market, however, is unable to ensure that all citizens will have access to primary and preventive health care, the obvious question arises, who is responsible for ensuring this right?

The Presbyterian Church resolved that only the federal government could be expected to undertake a project of this magnitude. After identifying the minimal limits for universal coverage, referred to as a "National Health Standard," this resolution even advocated a specific financing and delivery system that might be called managed competition with employer mandates. The resolution recommended that Congress enact legislation to assure universal access to health care through a three-step process:

[1] Requiring all employers, public and private, to provide insurance or direct coverage for all employees and their dependents for health care that meets or exceeds the National Health Standard.

[2] Amending all current governmental and publicly subsidized health care programs to meet or exceed the National Health Standard.

[3] Providing subsidized health care coverage meeting the National Health Standard for all persons not otherwise covered by [1] and [2] above.[9]

In other words, the proposal in *Life Abundant* foreshadows President Clinton's Health Security Act. Knowing that this document was sent to Governor William J. Clinton of Arkansas who happened to be chairing the "Governors' Task Force on Health Care Reform" in 1988, the similarities might seem less coincidental.

Three years later, however, the Presbyterian Church adopted a much bolder statement: "The 203rd General Assembly (1991) decries our nation's failure to establish an equitable, efficient, and universally accessible medical plan."[10] While this report claims to supplement, not to supplant, past recommendations regarding health care reform, the differences are significant. The 1991 report subtly dismissed managed competition and insisted upon a single payer system: "The least costly method for collecting the necessary funds to finance the health system should be used. We favor a national-level, progressive income tax for individuals and corporations as the most efficient system available at present. . . . Neither a retrospective, charge-based reimbursement system, nor a system in which all providers are employees of the National Medical Plan, is advisable."[11] Some Presbyterian leaders interpreted this resolution to mean that anything less than a single-payer system would be a failure.[12]

JUDAISM

Reform Jewish leaders were among the first to support universal health care coverage. In 1973, such convictions led the Union of American Hebrew Congregations (UAHC) to adopt, "Health Care and Health Insurance." This resolution advocates a "national comprehensive prepaid single benefit standard health insurance with no deductible, to cover prevention, treatment and rehabilitation in all fields of health care."[13] Twenty years later, the UAHC issued a follow-up resolution, "Reform of the Health Care System." This resolution advocated a single-payer system as the most likely means of achieving universal access to health care in the United States.[14]

INTERRELIGIOUS HEALTH CARE ACCESS CAMPAIGN

When Jimmy Carter was president, he had advocated universal access to health care, but he could not get sufficient support from a Democratic Congress to pursue this legislation in the midst of double-digit inflation and unemployment rates. Carter, an evangelical Christian who is often associated with the religious Left, believed that religious leaders could play a key role in mobilizing support for national legislation regarding health care reform. In 1989, former President Jimmy Carter invited 200 religious leaders from around the United States to the Carter Center along with politicians and health care experts. This was the origin of a group that began calling itself the Interreligious Health Care Access Campaign on January 7, 1992. By April of 1993, the National Council of Churches, virtually all Mainline Protestant and African American Protestant denominations, the historic peace churches, the Central Conference of American Rabbis, Network (a National Catholic Social Justice Lobby), and numerous other religious organizations had endorsed the Interreligious Access Health Care Access Campaign. The campaign lobbied Congress, testified before two congressional committees, and met twice a month with consumer advocates, labor unions, and Democratic proponents for health care reform.[15]

The Interreligious Health Care Access Campaign created "Working Principles for Assessing National Health Care Legislation."[16] Their first principle identifies their objective for reforming America's health care system.

"We seek a national health care plan which serves everyone living in the United States. Participation must not be limited due to discrimination on the basis of race, income, gender, geography (urban or rural), age disability, health status, sexual orientation, religion, country of origin, or legal status."[17] In short, they insist that everyone has the right to basic health care. Elaborating upon the minimal standards for a National Health Standard, they identify "pre- and post-natal care, immunizations and epidemiologic services. . . . Provision of early screening, diagnosis and treatment through physical examinations (inclusive of dental, eye, and hearing care. . . . Programs of extended care and rehabilitation. . . . Programs of mental health. . . ."[18] In fact, they proclaim, "The more benefits included in any single piece of legislation, the more positively we will regard that bill."[19]

Perhaps the most controversial part of their plan, however, is their proposed financing system. They proposed that the system be fully supported by federal funds that are acquired through progressive income taxes and by increasing taxes on "products and manufacturing methods that damage health."[20] In short, they insisted upon the single-payer system where government is the single payer.

These principles and accompanying videos were used for lobbying efforts aimed at political leaders and as a resource for educating people in local congregations. When Jimmy Carter was unable to convince them that a single-payer system was unrealistic, he distanced himself from the Interreligious Health Care Access Campaign and pointed out that their critiques would undermine President Clinton's proposal and serve to legitimate the status quo.

THE HEALTH SECURITY ACT

A Southern Baptist, Bill Clinton, won the 1992 presidential election by portraying himself as a "new Democrat" who had supported George Bush's policy during the Persian Gulf War, who discussed returning some federal powers back to the states, and who promised to "end welfare as we know it."[21] After 12 years of being shut out of the White House, the religious Left assumed that their voices would again have some influence on the president's policies. In particular, they focused upon the most progressive of Bill Clinton's objectives—health care reform.

President Bill Clinton's speeches on health care reform echoed the concerns of the religious Left. As its citizens debated the proposed "Health Security Act," the United States ranked twelfth in life expectancy, twenty-first in the number of deaths of children under age 5, twenty-second in infant mortality, and twenty-fourth in the percentage of babies born with inadequate birth weight.[22] Half of all two-year-olds were not receiving adequate immunizations.[23] Even though the United States is the only industrialized nation that does not guarantee universal access to health care, Americans spent more than 14 percent of their gross national product on health care while the citizens of no other nation spent more than 10 percent.[24] Health care costs were also rising between two and three times the rate of inflation, a faster rate than in any other nation.[25] Fifty-eight million Americans had no insurance.[26] Every month for the previous five years, about 100,000 Americans had lost their health care coverage.[27]

Clinton argued that failure to provide universal access to health care actually contributes to the disproportionately high costs of health care in the United States:

You're also paying . . . a significant premium because we are the only advanced country that permits some people just to say, "I won't have any insurance: I don't believe I'll be covered." But they all get health care if an emergency happens or when it's too late and they're too sick and they happen to show up at the emergency room. And then the cost is passed on to the rest of you in higher premiums. . . . Because we don't provide prescription drugs for elderly people in a lot of family policies, our hospital bills are much greater . . . [T]hey wind up getting care when it's too late, too expensive, and they're in the hospital. And it adds costs to the whole system.[28]

Hospitals must absorb or pass along over $25 billion worth of care for which they are not compensated each year.[29] As hospitals pass along those costs, insurance rates rise. As insurance rates rise, more companies and individuals forgo insurance. Because more people are without insurance, hospitals provide more care for which they are not directly compensated. Clinton claimed that any insurance reform that fell short of universal coverage would contribute to this vicious cycle.[30]

Clinton also argued that many citizens who do have insurance are locked into their current jobs by our existing health care system. "There are 81 million Americans—out of a population of 255 million—in families with preexisting conditions."[31] Rarely do insurance policies cover preexisting conditions, and then the costs are exorbitant. Therefore, employees are often given the difficult choice of staying in their current jobs with health care coverage or accepting a different job and losing health care coverage. The consequence is that nearly one-third of all U.S. citizens are locked into their current jobs at a time when typical individuals are expected to change jobs seven or eight times during the course of their careers. Under Clinton's proposal, individuals with preexisting conditions could not be refused coverage, nor would they have higher premiums.[32]

While some individuals are locked into current jobs because of our health care system, Clinton argued that others are locked out of the job market altogether. There are 49 million Americans with disabilities (24 million with severe disabilities). Half of these citizens have no health care coverage. Many employers will not hire persons with disabilities because that means the insurance companies will charge them higher rates. Consequently, many persons with disabilities can only receive health care coverage through

Medicaid and then only if they are poor. Clinton claimed that the message was all too clear: "You can have health benefits, but only if you spend yourself into poverty, and above all, you must not work."[33] Under Clinton's program, persons with disabilities and their employers could not be charged more for health care coverage by the insurance agencies. This would allow many persons with disabilities to join the workforce who must be poor to qualify for health care coverage in the current system.

In a similar argument, Clinton identified a connection between welfare and health care. After challenging the notion that welfare benefits serve as a positive motivation for staying on welfare,[34] he pointed out that most people on welfare have small children who receive primary and preventive medical care through Medicaid, which would be lost if they accepted a low-paying job.[35] Clinton claimed that guaranteeing health care coverage would allow many individuals who are currently on welfare to accept low-paying jobs and actually be better off than they are under our current health care system.

President Clinton argued that our current health care system is far from efficient, in part, because of the high administrative costs of health care anarchy. Because 1500 companies offer thousands of different insurance policies, health care providers must employ an inordinate number of people to read the fine print of these policies to see exactly who and what is covered.[36] Even then, they may be required to call an insurance company in advance to guarantee that they will be compensated for performing a basic medical procedure. From 1983 to 1993, the average hospital in the United States hired four times as many clerical workers as health care providers.[37] Clinton drew an analogy with Canada's health care system to illustrate the relatively wasteful costs of our system:

There was a recent study of two hospitals, one in Canada, one in the United States, with the same number of beds, the same vacancy rate, the same patient caseload. There were 200 people in the clerical department of the American hospital and 6 in the Canadian hospital.[38]

We are paying a significant amount of money for administrative costs that do not add to the quality of the health care.

Clinton argued that the Health Security Act would reduce the administrative costs in two ways. First, comprehensive benefits would be provided to all citizens, so there would be no questions about whether these procedures would be covered or not. Second, there would be a standard claims form for doctors, for hospitals, and for consumers that would simplify the paperwork bureaucracy.[39] Clinton summarized the 1342-page Health Security Act like this:

Here's my plan. First, guarantee everybody private health insurance. . . . Second, make sure the benefits are adequate, not just catastrophic health care but primary and preventive health care, too. . . . Third, have insurance reforms [to reduce the administrative costs of the current system]. . . . Fourth . . . leave Medicare the

way it is: it's working. But extend the benefits to elderly people to include a benefit of prescription drugs . . . and [cover] long-term care in the home and in the
community.[40]

In short, the Health Security Act would have provided a federal guarantee
of access to primary and preventive health care for all citizens and eliminated some administrative costs of the current system (while creating new
administrative costs).

Clinton then summarized the most politically divisive feature of his program, the proposed financing system:

If we want to cover everybody, we only have two choices. You look all around
the world: there are only two options. [1] You either have to do it through a
Government-funded program, like Medicare for everybody—abolish all insurance,
charge everybody a tax and fund it—[2] or you have to have insurance for everybody.[41]

Clinton proposed the second option and called his system "managed competition with employer mandates."

Clinton appealed to simplicity and to realism in proposing managed competition with employer mandates:

It seems to me that the fairest and simplest, and, if you will, the most conservative
way to achieve universal coverage, to have health care security for everybody, is to
ask employers and employees who aren't doing anything or barely doing anything
to do more so that they can fulfill their own responsibilities and then use tax funds
to cover the unemployed, uninsured people for whom you could say, "Well there's
a general responsibility just like Medicare and Medicaid" and then organize the
market so that smaller businesses and self-employed people, (a) get discounts if they
need it [sic] and (b) are able to buy good insurance on the same terms that those of
us who are insured by Government or larger businesses can.[42]

Clearly, part of Clinton's strategy in selling the Health Security Act to the
American people was to distinguish it from "socialized medicine" and to
downplay the role of the federal government in funding and implementing
this program.

Clinton recognized that the Health Security Act would not be perfect. At
the beginning of the reform process, he claimed that it would be a realistic
tool for promoting relative justice:

Legitimate objections can be raised to any course of action in this area. That is, there
is no such thing as a perfect solution. So whatever course we choose to take, some-
body can say, "Well, it's not perfect for these reasons." To that, I have two
answers. . . . Number one, the worst thing we can do is to keep on doing what
we're doing now, because more and more people are falling out of the system and
the cost is becoming more and more burdensome to those who are still bearing
it. . . . Number two, this is not going to be the end of the line. Whatever problems

are there can be fixed later. But we will never, never get anywhere if we stand para-lyzed, because there's no such thing as a perfect alternative.[43]

Advocating a pragmatic strategy for providing universal access to health care, President Clinton expected the Left, and particularly the religious Left, to support his agenda.

Before looking at the response of religious communities to Clinton's pro-posed legislation, however, it is important to understand how the public pol-icy debates over health care turned into an abortion debate. In the context of determining which procedures should be covered in a National Health Stan-dard, pro-choice forces insisted that access to abortion be recognized as a basic human right to be covered by taxpayers' money. The Religious Coali-tion for Reproductive Rights, for example, insisted that any new health plan "offers full reproductive health services, including contraception, abortion, pre- and post-natal care, and voluntary sterilization."[44] Many of the organi-zations associated with the Religious Coalition for Reproductive Rights also identify with the National Council of Churches and the Interreligious Health Care Access Campaign. Pro-life forces, on the other hand, insisted that no per-son should be coerced by the state to receive an abortion, to perform an abor-tion, or even to pay one cent in taxes that might be used for abortions. In the context of the contemporary culture wars, President Clinton chose to include abortion as one of the procedures to be covered, thus alienating the Roman Catholic Church, the National Association of Evangelicals, and others.

RESPONSES FROM THE INTERRELIGIOUS HEALTH CARE ACCESS CAMPAIGN

Lobbyists on behalf of the Interreligious Health Care Access Campaign met with Bruce Fried and other Clinton administrators. Clinton's adminis-trators claimed that the primary objectives of the Interreligious Health Care Access Campaign would be met through the Health Security Act. The stick-ing point remained the question of financing: single payer versus managed competition. Clinton had made his position clear: because a single-payer system is unacceptable to the vast majority of U.S. citizens and legislators, it could not be seriously entertained. Leaders of the Interreligious Health Care Access Campaign refused to compromise on this issue until two weeks before Congress was to adjourn. They exhausted their resources trying to engage in insider lobbying to persuade members of Congress to support a more radical plan than the one proposed by President Clinton.

RESPONSES BY THE NATIONAL COUNCIL OF CHURCHES

The National Council of Churches (NCC) was one of the principal sup-porters of the Interreligious Health Care Access Campaign. Not surpris-ingly, the NCC also failed to mobilize grassroots support for the Health

Security Act. In November of 1993, the leaders of the NCC sent a letter to President Clinton that praised him for his efforts to guarantee universal access to health care. They claimed, "Our commitment is, first and foremost, to universal coverage, without which America's most vulnerable citizens will continue to live in a state of health carelessness."[45] The same letter encouraged President Clinton to serve "everybody through a single system of health care provision with one payment process."[46] David Anderson keenly identifies the political implications of this letter:

While praising the Clinton effort, the council leaders said they would retain the right to criticize the administration and work for modifications they think appropriate. Many church activists involved in health care reform favor the "single-payer" system, such as that in Canada, rather than the "managed competition" plan proposed by Clinton that would continue a modified private insurance system.[47]

In short, the National Council of Churches typified the Mainline Protestant leaders' response to the Health Security Act—lukewarm support because it did not go far enough.

ROMAN CATHOLIC RESPONSES

Unlike the Mainline Protestant leaders, Roman Catholic bishops seemed willing to support managed competition with employer mandates as a strategy for financing the health care system. Nevertheless, the politics of abortion prevented the Catholic bishops from supporting President Clinton's Health Security Act. In June of 1993, the National Conference of Catholic Bishops issued a 10-page resolution reaffirming the church's position that health care is a basic human right. With respect to financing the new health care system, the Catholic bishops were very accommodating. They would not insist upon employer mandates or a single-payer system. Bishop O'Donnell, who helped to draft the resolution, claimed that the bishops did not wish "to be so precise we don't have room for maneuvering."[48] Clearly, the bishops considered the issue of financing to be a matter of prudence, not moral principle.

The inclusion of abortion as a medical treatment to be covered as part of the National Health Standard, however, proved to be the sticking point for the Catholic bishops. They warned:

As longtime advocates of health care reforms, we appeal to the leaders of the nation to avoid a divisive and polarizing dispute. . . . The common good is not advanced when advocates of so-called 'choice' compel taxpayers to fund what we and many others are convinced is the destruction of human life.[49]

The "consistent ethic of life," which simultaneously motivates them to support health care reform and to oppose abortion, led to the possibility of conflicting agendas. In this case, the issue of abortion would appear to be the highest priority of the National Conference of Catholic Bishops. The bishops lobbied extremely hard to keep abortion out of Clinton's plan. Collectively and individually, they wrote letters, issued resolutions, met with congressional leaders, presented speeches, and gave sermons. They even sent out 19 million postcards noting their disapproval of the Clinton proposal's inclusion of abortion.[50]

Of course, many American Catholics disagree with the church's official position on abortion.[51] Still others question the priority abortion receives within Catholic social ethics. For example, James E. Hug, executive director of the Jesuit Center of Concern, argued, "Abortion has to be seen as important, but not the only important issue. Abortion is not the only thing that kills. To sacrifice the health care reform on the altar of abortion would be a tragedy."[52]

In an attempt to find common ground between pro-choice and pro-life advocates, the Senate Finance Committee articulated a "conscience clause" that would allow any employer or health plan to refuse to buy or provide abortion coverage for religious or moral reasons. The bishops rejected this plan, claiming, "abortion rights would be greatly expanded from the current law, which denies federally financed abortions for poor women."[53] Pro-choice organizations, on the other hand, argued that such a clause would undermine universal access to health care. If such a religious clause were included, they argued, employers could refuse to cover other procedures, from circumcisions to blood transfusions, by simply claiming religious exemptions. In short, neither side seemed willing to compromise or find common ground on the abortion issue in order to salvage health care reform.

EVANGELICALS

Many evangelical leaders rejected the Health Security Act, not only for its coverage of abortion but also for expanding the power of federal government. Some organizations, like the National Association of Evangelicals and the Southern Baptist Convention, seemed open to reforms with a limited role for the federal government. In March of 1994, the National Association of Evangelicals drafted a resolution that supported universal coverage, but they called for "health care provisions which will maximize the creativity of the private sector while minimizing governmental control."[54] Moreover, they insisted, even more sharply than the Catholic bishops, that they would oppose any plan that included coverage for abortion.

The Southern Baptist Convention adopted a similar resolution in June of 1994. First, they stated that it must contain sufficient "conscience clauses" to protect religious people and organizations from participating in "morally objectionable" health practices, such as abortion.[55] Second, they stated that the Baptist "heritage of insistence on limited government causes us to

believe the need for reform does not mandate a government-controlled
health care system."[56] In short, they flatly rejected the single-payer system
advocated by Mainline Protestants but seemed willing to consider a program financed through managed competition with employer mandates.
When President Clinton included abortion in the Health Security Act, the
Southern Baptist Convention clearly opposed his proposal.

The Christian Coalition did not need to know how the abortion issue
would be resolved to determine its stance on the Health Security Act. Ralph
Reed explained, "We seek a pro-family, *free-market alternative* to health
care reform [emphasis added]."[57] Ralph Reed went on to argue that Clinton was advocating socialized medicine, that Clinton's proposals would
lead to the rationing of health care, that the proposal would require increasing taxes and/or raising the national debt, and that U.S.-based corporations
would become even less capable of competing in the global marketplace.
Given these conclusions, the Christian Coalition spent $1.4 million in its
campaign to defeat universal access to health care.[58] At the time, opposing
the Health Security Act was the largest lobbying effort conducted by the
Christian Coalition to date.

The Christian Coalition, along with other groups who lobbied against
the Health Security Act, had a profound impact upon public opinion. As
late as July of 1994, 69 percent of the American public supported health
care reform while only 26 percent preferred the existing system.[59] One
month later, only 39 percent supported health care reform.[60]

FALLACIES REVISITED

Three fallacies of wartime logic might help to expose the tragedy that
religious leaders seemed more interested in winning the culture wars than
improving the lives of actually existing individuals. In the heat of battle, the
arguments of the religious Left and the religious Right often looked like
mirror images of each other.

If Right Is Good, Further Right Is Better; or If Left Is Good, Further Left Is Better

Assuming that if capitalism is good then *laissez faire* capitalism is better,
the Christian Coalition argued that government has no responsibility to
ensure the health of its citizens. They ignored the problems with the current
health care system. Refusing to allow empirical evidence to stand in the way
of ideology, they concluded that good, hardworking citizens would have
their health care needs met if government would just get out of the way.

Assuming that capitalism cannot be reformed, the Interreligious Health
Care Access Campaign advocated a single-payer system that seemed
extremely unpopular, not only among the American public but even among

their lay constituency. They lacked the political realism to support a policy that would have promoted a greater degree of relative justice. Refusing to allow the public discourse to influence their public policy pronouncements, these religious leaders concluded that health care could only be more equitable if it were financed through progressive income taxes.

Either You Are for Us or against Us

Both the Interreligious Health Care Access Campaign and the Christian Coalition dismissed managed competition with employer mandates. Both argued that there is no middle ground between socialism and capitalism. They saw no common ground and no room for compromise. Managed competition with employer mandates is an ideological compromise. It recognizes systemic inequalities resulting from the free market and seeks to provide a safety net. It also recognizes the potentially bureaucratic nature of government programs, so it allows private health insurance companies to compete so that the most efficient companies will be rewarded with the highest profits. Whether the Health Security Act represented the best or the worst of both extremes is certainly open to debate, but there was precious little room for debate in 1994.

The Catholic bishops were willing to support managed competition with employer mandates. In this regard, they seemed prepared to transcend the contemporary culture wars in order to contribute to the vital center of U.S. public policy. On the other hand, the Catholic bishops and their pro-choice opponents could not compromise or find common ground on the issue of abortion. The type of compromises worked out in the Senate Finance Committee could have taken abortion from the center to the margins of health care reform debates.

The Enemy of My Enemy Must Be My Friend

The contemporary culture wars create surprising coalitions. In their efforts to oppose Marxism, the Christian Right often resonates with Nietzsche, Sumner, Spencer, and other Social Darwinists. In their efforts to distance themselves from the Christian Right, the Christian Left imitates the most utopian elements of Marxist social theories. During the debates surrounding health care reform, cultural warriors seemed more interested in destroying their ideological enemies than improving the health of actually existing individuals. In the process, they distorted their own traditions in ways that would have seemed tragic to their predecessors.

CONCLUSIONS

Had religious leaders been less interested in winning the culture wars and more interested in adopting pragmatic, prophetic responses that contribute to the vital center of U.S. policy, they might have been able to improve America's health care system. My optimism about how religious communities might contribute to the discussion of health care reform in the future may seem unwarranted in light of recent American politics, but the unresolved crisis of health care in America will not disappear any time soon. Minor legislation has passed (the Health Insurance Portability Act, the Mental Health Parity Act, and the Kassebaum-Kennedy bill, among others), but the health care crisis will apparently get worse before America's religious leaders are willing to engage in the kind of compromises necessary to promote relative justice. For 50 years, Mainline Protestant, Catholic, and Jewish leaders have been calling access to health care a basic human right. In the heat of the culture wars, however, these religious leaders failed to act prudently to support health care reforms. Instead of mobilizing support for President Clinton's Health Security Act, the religious Left helped to undermine health care reforms.

NOTES

1. National Conference of Catholic Bishops, "Health and Health Care," in *Pastoral Letters of the United States Catholic Bishops* 4, ed. Hugh J. Nolan (Washington, D.C.: United States Catholic Conference, 1984), 469.

2. Ibid. They also noted the significant contributions of the Catholic Church to America's health care system. "Today our country is served by a variety of Catholic health care facilities: more than six hundred twenty short-term hospitals, some two hundred sixty long-term care facilities, four schools of medicine, one hundred and seventy nursing schools, and numerous institutions providing research and education in the health care field," 476.

3. Ibid., 484.

4. Ibid.

5. Ibid.

6. Ibid.

7. Ibid., 484–85.

8. Presbyterian Church (U.S.A.), *Life Abundant: Values, Choices, and Health Care: The Responsibility and Role of the Presbyterian Church (U.S.A)* (Louisville: Office of the General Assembly, 1988), 17.

9. Ibid., 28.

10. Presbyterian Church (U.S.A.), *Resolution on Christian Responsibility and a National Medical Plan* (Louisville: Office of the General Assembly), 1.

11. Ibid., 26–27.

12. David Zuverink, interview by author, telephone, 9 March 1995.

13. Union of American Hebrew Congregations, "Health Care and Health Insurance," (Washington D.C.: Religious Action Center of Reform Judaism, 1973), 1.

14. Union of American Hebrew Congregations, "Reform of the Health Care System," (Washington D.C.: Religious Action Center of Reform Judaism, 1993), 1.

15. Nancy Chupp, "Health Care Reform: What Kind?," *Christian Social Action* 4 (February 1993), 33.

16. Interreligious Health Care Access Campaign, *Working Principles for Assessing National Health Care Legislation* (Washington, D.C.: Author, 1992).

17. Ibid., 3.

18. Ibid., 3–4.

19. Ibid., 4.

20. Ibid., 4–7.

21. See Cathleen Decker, "Clinton Details His Plan for Welfare Reform," *Los Angeles Times* (10 September 1992), A1.

22. Chupp, "Health Care Reform," 28.

23. William J. Clinton, "Address before a Joint Session of Congress on Administration Goals: February 17, 1993," *Weekly Compilation of Presidential Documents* 29, no. 7 (22 February 1993): 219.

24. Clinton, *Presidential Documents* 30, no. 28 (18 July 1994): 1479.

25. Clinton, *Presidential Documents* 29, no. 37 (20 September 1993): 1781.

26. Clinton, *Presidential Documents* 30, no. 19 (16 May 1994): 1033.

27. Clinton, *Presidential Documents* 30, no. 39 (3 October 1994): 1868.

28. Clinton, *Presidential Documents* 30, no. 16 (25 April 1994): 828–29.

29. Clinton, *Presidential Documents* 30, no. 5 (7 February 1994): 181.

30. Clinton, *Presidential Documents* 30, no. 30 (1 August 1994): 1543.

31. Clinton, *Presidential Documents* 30, no. 19 (16 May 1994): 1033.

32. Clinton, *Presidential Documents* 30, no. 19 (16 May 1994): 1046. This issue was partially resolved through the "Health Insurance Portability and Accountability Act," passed by Congress in 1996, but the qualifications and expenses are likely to exclude poorer families in particular.

33. Clinton, *Presidential Documents* 30, no. 18 (2 May 1994): 954.

34. Clinton, *Presidential Documents* 30, no. 5 (7 February 1994): 181.

35. Ibid., 183.

36. Clinton, *Presidential Documents* 30, no. 16 (25 April 1994): 830.

37. Clinton, *Presidential Documents* 29, no. 29 (20 September 1993): 1776.

38. Clinton, *Presidential Documents* 30, no. 16, (25 April 1994): 828.

39. Clinton, *Presidential Documents* 29, no. 30 (27 September 1993): 1864.

40. Clinton, *Presidential Documents* 30, no. 16 (25 April 1994): 829–30.

41. Ibid., 829–30.

42. Clinton, *Presidential Documents* 30, no. 19 (16 May 1994): 1048.

43. Clinton, *Presidential Documents* 29, no. 4 (1 February 1993): 98.

44. Andrew Mollison, "Health Care Reform: Religion Mixes with Politics in Debate over New System," *The Atlanta Journal and Constitution* (26 February 1994), C4.

45. David E. Anderson, "Council Stands on Health Care," *Petersburg Times* (20 November 1993), 5.

46. Ibid.

47. Ibid.

48. Peter Steinfels, "Bishops Pass Resolution Warning Against Abortion in Health Plan," *New York Times* (19 June 1993), 1,47. In fact, the Canadian bishops have played a significant role in supporting Canada's single-payer system. See P. Travis Kroeker, *Christian Ethics and Political Economy in North America: A Critical Analysis* (Montreal: McGill-Queens University Press, 1995), 104–11.

49. Ibid.

50. John W. Kennedy, "RX for America," *Christianity Today* (25 April 1994), 40.

51. A Catholic woman is 29 percent more likely to get an abortion than a Protestant woman. Moreover, one-fifth of all women in the United States who receive abortions identify themselves as "born-again" or Evangelical Christians. See Barbara Vobejda, "Abortion Reaches Wide Cross Section of Women; Study of U.S. Patients Seeking Procedure Finds Many Belong to Religious Groups that Oppose It," *The Washington Post* (8 August 1996), A17.

52. Rick Allen, "Jesuit Group Urges Moral Public Policy," *Washington Post* (22 May 1993), G10.

53. Karen Hosler, "Abortion Issue Threatens to Torpedo Health Reform," *Baltimore Sun* (14 July 1994), 1A.

54. John Dart, "Groups Debate Clinton Health Plan; Politics: Christian Coalition in Studio City Calls Proposal Anti-family. Clergy Network Luncheon in Reseda says 'Everybody Should Be Covered.' " *Los Angeles Times* (26 March 1994), B:11.

55. Kathryn Rogers, "S. Baptists Back Health Care Change," *St. Louis Post-Dispatch* (16 June 1994), 3C.

56. Ibid.

57. Darrell Holland, "Religious Leaders Support Health Reform; Pat Robertson's Opposition Campaign Draws Criticism," *Plain Dealer* (9 April 1994), 8F.

58. Ibid.

59. David W. Moore, "Public Firm on Health Reform Goals," *The Gallup Poll Monthly* (July 1994), 12.

60. Lydia Saad, "Public Has Cold Feet on Health Care Reform," *The Gallup Poll Monthly* (August 1994), 2.

6

Welfare Reform

For some, the Reagan revolution marked the beginning of genuine welfare reform. The presidential victory of Democratic President Bill Clinton in 1992, they concluded, was a minor setback in the movement to restore America's free market system, in part, by dismantling the New Deal programs. In 1994, the American people demonstrated an obvious preference for Republican candidates by giving them a majority in the House of Representatives for the first time in 40 years. These Republicans, working hand in hand with the New Christian Right, claimed that the American people had given them a mandate that was quite different from the liberal policy proposals such as the Health Security Act being advanced by the Clinton administration.

Although George Gilder, Marvin Olasky, Charles Murray, Pat Robertson, and Gary North, among others, had already identified welfare as the source of poverty and immorality in America, the two most "public" documents in favor of cutting the welfare state are the *Contract with America* and the *Contract with the American Family*. The similarity in title between these documents is not coincidental. Ralph Reed, executive director of the Christian Coalition, held a press conference in the U.S. capitol where he was joined by Newt Gingrich and many of the Republican representatives who had signed the *Contract with America*. Among other things, the *Contract with the American Family* identifies the problem of welfare in the same terms:

The welfare system has caused the work ethic of the lowest income groups to collapse and family breakup and illegitimacy to soar. . . . This social tragedy is the direct result of our current welfare system which rewards people for not working by giving them numerous benefits and penalizes those who return to work by taking away the benefits.[1]

The *Contract with the American Family* was an unabashed attempt to identify the welfare reform policy advocated by the Republican Party as a "Christian" imperative.

The welfare reform policy advocated by the Republican representatives in the *Contract with America* is called the "Personal Responsibility Act." It assumes that the obstacles to employment are laziness, idleness, and irresponsibility. It assumes that poor people would become responsible if they were not given an unfailing provision by the government. It assumes that teenage girls choose to get pregnant so they can live on welfare. These assumptions are made explicit:

Government programs designed to give a helping hand to the neediest of Americans have instead bred illegitimacy, crime, illiteracy, and more poverty. Our *Contract with America* will change this destructive social behavior by requiring welfare recipients to take personal responsibility for the decisions they make. Our *Contract* will achieve what some thirty years of massive welfare spending has not been able to accomplish; reduce illegitimacy, require work, and save taxpayers money.[2]

Thus, the *Contract with America* describes its proposal as a winning solution for all. Hardworking American citizens can retain more of the fruits of their labor. With a little tough love, the poor will soon be living productive lives of dignity. Children will benefit by being born into healthy families with productive parents.

Anticipating the argument by their critics that cutting funding will not deter pregnancy, they declare:

Republicans understand one important thing ignored by most Democrats— incentives affect behavior. Currently, the federal government provides young girls the following deal: Have an illegitimate baby and taxpayers will guarantee you cash, food stamps, and medical care, plus a host of other benefits worth a minimum of $12,000 per year ($3000 more than a full-time job paying minimum wage). It's time to change the incentive and make responsible parenthood the norm and not the exception.[3]

Young women, they claim, make a rational choice to get pregnant so that they can enjoy the benefits of welfare. Attempts to improve the standard of living for the working poor are futile, they conclude, so the obvious solution is to remove the option of living on welfare or to make life on welfare less comfortable.

Expanding upon their attempt to promote healthy families, the *Contract with America* seeks to discourage illegitimacy by denying AFDC payments to unmarried mothers under 18 years old (or up to 20 years old at the discretion of state legislators) and by requiring mothers to name the father of the child in order to qualify for AFDC payments (except in cases of rape and incest).[4] Noting that single mothers often bear the burden of poverty, the *Contract with America* claims that they want also to hold fathers accountable.

Because they contend that liberal attempts to remove the "obstacles" to employment for the poor are naïve and impractical, they point to the alternative, tough love. They contend that welfare must be viewed as a temporary response to hardships, not as a way of life. Therefore, they proposed a limit of two consecutive years and a total of five years for AFDC payments.[5] To offer unlimited entitlements based on need, they contend, is to perpetuate dependency, to encourage idleness, to promote poverty.

Anticipating criticism that their tough-love approach is too callous, they point to the results of the naïve sentimental, and utopian programs associated with the Democratic Party since 1963:

Johnson's War on Poverty has been an unqualified failure. Despite spending trillions of dollars, it has had the unintended consequence of making welfare more attractive than work to many families, and once welfare recipients become dependent on public assistance, they are caught in the now-familiar welfare trap.[6]

Yet, they concede that their targets are not only those programs that had been created after 1963. The central focus of their efforts was Aid to Families with Dependent Children. "Established in 1935 under the Social Security Act, AFDC was created to help widows care for their children. It now serves divorced, deserted, and never married individuals and their children."[7] Such distinctions are important, they imply, in discerning between the deserving poor and those who are just plain irresponsible.

To demonstrate that they are interested in eliminating some of the obstacles that keep poor people poor, they emphasize the importance of education:

To help combat illiteracy, states may reduce AFDC payments by up to $75 per month to mothers under the age of twenty-one who have not completed high school or earned their high school equivalency. Payments may also be reduced if a dependent child does not maintain minimum school attendance.[8]

By reducing welfare benefits for uneducated people, they contend, they can encourage poor people to develop the education necessary to be competitive in the free market.

Anticipating the argument from their most vocal constituents that these proposals do not go far enough, they point out that humble agenda is but the beginning. "It represents the first substantive steps on the road to a smaller government with lower taxes and fewer regulations."[9]

Religious Right Responses to the Contracts

Columnist Don Feder was among the first religious Right activists to respond to the *Contract with America*. He would elaborate upon the significance of the Republican Party's attack on the AFDC program:

The cash isn't all that much. Nationwide it's about $25 billion a year; that's about 1.5 percent of the federal budget. In some years of the 1980s, the nation spent more on farm subsidies. . . . People getting AFDC usually get Medicaid and food stamps, and often help with housing, so the actual financial burden is more. But it's not going to break the bank.[10]

For Feder and others, morality, not short-term economic interests, lies at the root of the welfare reform debates. "The real cost of welfare is that it takes away all incentives for responsible behavior," he explains.[11]

After taking a lashing by the American public for the callousness of some of their proposals, Republican representatives greeted Marvin Olasky's *The Tragedy of American Compassion* with a sense of reassurance. In 1996, Olasky changed the tone of his work by calling it *Renewing American Compassion,* for which Newt Gingrich wrote the introduction. Olasky argues against "the centralizing impulses of the 1930s and 1960s. We need to turn to the future by giving up our twentieth-century mistakes, picking up what was best in nineteenth-century understanding, and making that vision work for tomorrow."[12]

Olasky concludes his book with an exegesis of scriptures to revitalize the spirits of welfare reformers. Pointing to the book of Proverbs, he insists, "character and economic success go together."[13] He points to the story of Exodus to proclaim, "there is no 'preferential option' for either poor or rich. God is a theological determinist and belief is more important than status."[14] He appeals to Paul to argue, only widows over 60 years old who have been faithful to their husbands should be identified among the truly needy.[15] Olasky also clarifies the meaning behind Jesus' statement, "Whatever you have done to the least of your brethren, you have done also to me":

Today's poor in the United States are the victims and perpetrators of illegitimacy and abandonment, family nonformation and malformation, alienation and loneliness and much else—but they are not suffering thirst, hunger, or nakedness, except by choice, insanity, or parental abuse. When we lack discernment, we give money to panhandlers that most often goes for drugs or alcohol. Christ does not include in his list of commended charitable acts, "When I was strung out you gave me dope."[16]

Olasky's words of encouragement to the martyrs of welfare reform, he explains, were inspired by Congress' 1995 welfare reform debates where the "religious Left . . . twisted Scripture to make it conform to modern liberal ideology."[17]

Catholic Responses to the Contracts

Cardinal John O'Connor, who has often been characterized in the media as a Republican partisan for his routine condemnations of pro-choice Democrats, surprised many people by blasting the welfare proposals of the *Contract with America*. Among other things, O'Connor argued that the proposal would lead to an "increased number of abortions."[18] Congressman Christopher Smith, former director of the New Jersey Right to Life Committee concurred, and he added, "I don't think you should use the child as a pawn in trying to influence the mother's behavior. These proposals are inhumane."[19]

The Administrative Board of the U.S. Catholic Conference responded to the *Contract with America* with a statement entitled, "Moral Principles and Policy Priorities for Welfare Reform." It would claim:

We are not defenders of the welfare status quo, which sometimes relies on bureaucratic approaches, discourages work, and breaks up families. However, we oppose abandonment of the Federal Government's necessary role in helping families overcome poverty and meet their children's basic needs. . . . Genuine welfare reform should rely on incentives more than harsh penalties.[20]

Given the history of Catholic social teaching, it is not surprising that they would criticize these proposals for failing to understand the causes of poverty.

Cleveland Catholic Bishop Anthony Pilla responded to "a certain meanness" in the current dialogue about welfare reform. He rejected the implication that poverty is a small phenomenon only suffered by the imprudent. After pointing to the poverty rates in his own diocese (13.9 percent in Lorain County, 14 percent in Summit County, 20 percent in Cuyahoga County, and 42.2 percent in Cleveland), he claimed, "You see that there is a great sense of urgency for us as we begin the work of building new cities of justice and peace."[21]

Cardinal Roger Mahony stated the case even more bluntly. "We are witnessing an extraordinary assault upon the poorest members of our society, blaming them not only for their personal plight and poverty but also for many of the other economic and social ills affecting our country."[22]

Bishop John Ricard argued that the bishops "should oppose a national retreat in the struggle against poverty. . . . We're for welfare reform but against punitive measures which hurt children and encourage abortion."[23]

Before the 1996 presidential election, the Catholic bishops issued their quadrennial statement on religion and politics. Because similar statements since 1976 had been interpreted as partisan support for the Republican Party (by focusing upon abortion), because the Christian Coalition had created a new organization called the Catholic Alliance to encourage Catholics to vote Republican, and because the majority of white Catholics voted for a Republican Congress in 1994 for the first time in over 150 years, the bishops' statement declared, "The challenge for our church is to be principled without being ideological, to be political without being partisan, to be civil without being soft, to be involved without being used."[24] Therefore, they proclaimed:

We stand with the unborn and the undocumented when many politicians seem to be abandoning them. We defend children in the womb and on welfare. We oppose the violence of abortion and the vengeance of capital punishment. We oppose assault weapons in our streets and condoms in our schools.[25]

The U.S. Catholic Bishops sought to emphasize their "consistent ethic of life." The clear implication is that they preferred the Democratic platform on some issues and the Republican platform on others, but they could not endorse either heartily.

Mainline Protestant Responses to the Contracts

In a statement entitled "Caring for People Receiving Welfare," the Office for Church in Society of the United Church of Christ responded to the *Contract with America* by stating "We are deeply concerned that in the contemporary debate over welfare, some of our Christian brothers and sisters have joined the chorus of hostility and have bought into some of the unfounded stereotypes about people who receive welfare."[26]

In a series of "Policy Alerts," the Episcopal Public Policy Network encouraged Episcopalians to persuade their elected officials that the proposed legislation is unacceptable:

The Personal Responsibility Act of 1995 recently passed the House. This legislation would be extremely harmful to poor children, teen mothers, and legal immigrants. It would not provide recipients with the tools they need to gain self-sufficiency. It also sets the stage for a harmful competition among States to provide the least benefits.[27]

No longer the "Republican Party at Prayer," the leadership of the Episcopal Church encouraged its members to "work toward a welfare system that lifts people out of poverty, not simply off of welfare rolls."[28]

The Evangelical Lutheran Church in America (ELCA) formed the Task Force on Economic Life. Though their study guide was not officially released until October of 1996, too late to influence the weighty legislative battles of 1996, it is clearly a reaction to the type of proposals presented in the *Contract with America*. It appeals to scriptural and theological resources to identify an uncritical faith in the free market as a form of idolatry:

We cannot ignore how a market system operates. However, if we allow it to become a system of unchallenged absolutes, we fall into idolatry. . . . From the perspective of our faith, economic activity and its results should be accountable to God's ongoing plan for humankind and the rest of creation.[29]

It then goes on to describe God's plan by distinguishing between the needs of the poor and the wants of the rich, warning that "self-interest can turn into a radical individualism," challenging people not to be greedy, and claiming that some people will be poor "due to factors outside their control."[30]

With a dramatic graph showing the "Average After-tax Income Gains and Losses between 1977 and 1992 by Various Family Groups," the ELCA study guide illustrates how the rich had gotten richer and the poor had gotten poorer under the administrations of Reagan and Bush: the poorest fifth of all Americans saw their incomes decline by 17 percent, the second poorest fifth saw their incomes decline by 7 percent, the middle fifth saw their incomes increase by one percent, the next richest fifth saw their incomes increase by 6 percent, the richest fifth saw their incomes increase by 28 percent, and the top one percent saw their incomes increase by 91 percent.[31] Putting this growing income inequality into a larger context, they report, "Those in the top 5 percent, whose annual incomes are more than $120,000, now take a bigger share of the national income than do the bottom 50 percent put together."[32]

The ELCA study guide also emphasizes the growing inequality of wealth in America. "In 1976, the wealthiest one percent owned 19 percent of private wealth. By 1995 this increased to 40 percent with the top 10 percent owning 71 percent."[33] Putting this level of inequality into a global framework, they point out, "The inequality gap in the United States today is wider than in any other developed nation."[34] Elaborating upon how social inequalities have harmed American children, they claim, "In 1994, the percent of children living in poverty in the U.S. was at its highest in thirty years. Nearly 16 million children—one in every four—live in poverty."[35]

The National Council of Churches has also responded to the type of welfare reform proposals offered in the *Contract with America* through the speeches of its leadership, most notably Joan Brown Campbell,[36] and through a study guide, *Advocating Justice and Equity: A Policy Resource Guide on Welfare, Work and Economic Policy.* Like the ELCA guide, it came out too late to influence the 1996 debates, but it seems to fairly reflect the NCC position. For example, the outside cover of the guide includes the following observations: "Since 1970 the pay gap in America has grown so wide that it threatens, as it did in the Great Depression, the social stability of the country. . . . Biblical and church tradition are clear that poverty is not a mark of having sinned but a result of being sinned against."[37]

Jewish Responses to the Contracts

On January 26, 1995, the United Synagogue of Conservative Judaism issued a Position Paper on Welfare Reform claiming that they would support genuine welfare reform but argued, "Welfare benefits must be restructured to 'make work pay,' such that no family with at least one full-time worker will be in poverty."[38] Responding to the proposals in the *Contract with America,* they claimed "arbitrary time limits on the receipt of AFDC benefits in the absence of guaranteed jobs represent an unacceptable 'tear in the social safety net.' "[39]

The Religious Action Center of Reform Judaism also rejected the type of legislation advocated in the *Contract with America.* Speaking on behalf of the Reform Jewish community, David Saperstein claimed, "[T]he moral test of any society is what its economic and social policies do for the most vulnerable of God's children. . . . This legislation fails that test."[40] Explaining what kind of welfare would pass that test, Rabbi Saperstein says, "when welfare 'reforms' ensure a guarantee of child care, job training, health care, and nutrition assistance to help move people out of poverty and into long-term self-sufficiency."[41]

Joint Responses to the Contracts

On November 8, 1995, prominent leaders from the Roman Catholic Church, the National Council of Churches, the Congress of National Black Churches, the Union of American Hebrew Congregations, and the Synagogue Council of America issued a joint statement criticizing the Republican welfare reform proposal and urging President Clinton not to sign it. "Unholy legislation that destroys the safety net must not be signed into law by President Clinton. . . . The very soul of our nation is at risk."[42]

PERSONAL RESPONSIBILITY AND WORK OPPORTUNITY RECONCILIATION ACT

On July 3, 1996, Democrat President Bill Clinton agreed to sign the Personal Responsibility and Work Opportunity Reconciliation Act (PRWORA). It represented somewhat of a compromise between the Personal Responsibility Act advocated by the House Republicans' *Contract with America* and Bill Clinton's proposal, though Clinton had to bend much further than the Republican House.[43] The stated goal of the PRWORA of 1996 is to "require work, promote parental responsibility and give states the flexibility to run programs that will help families turn welfare checks into paychecks."[44]

The PRWORA abolished the AFDC program, thus ending a 60 year federal guarantee of aid to America's poor. In its stead, the PRWORA created block grants to states for Temporary Assistance for Needy Families (TANF). Whereas AFDC provided states with unlimited federal funding on a matching basis, TANF will cap the block grants to states based on past spending. Moreover, the states are allowed to reduce their contributions by 20 percent to 25 percent.[45] This legislation does encourage states to

improve child care access for welfare recipients, though it offers no guar-
antees.[46] Other key features of this legislation include:

- TANF cannot be provided for more than five cumulative years (less if the state so desires), regardless of need.[47]
- States must require families to work after two years on assistance.
- States may choose to cap benefits when a TANF recipient has another child.
- Unmarried minor parents are required to live with an adult or in an adult-supervised setting.
- Single mothers who fail to cooperate with paternity establishment will have their monthly cash assistance reduced by at least 25 percent.
- States can compete for a bonus by demonstrating that their policies have decreased the number of out-of-wedlock births and abortions.
- States may require recipients to write "Individual Responsibility Plans."
- Individuals who are convicted of drug-related felonies are prohibited for life from receiving benefits from the TANF and food stamp programs.[48]
- States may terminate Medicaid eligibility for adults who are terminated from TANF for failure to work.
- Legal immigrants are no longer eligible for the Supplemental Security Income or food stamps.[49]
- States may choose to make legal immigrants ineligible for Medicaid, TANF, WIC, and any other state-funded assistance until citizenship is granted.
- Federal and state officials must report illegal aliens to the Department of Immigration and Naturalization Services.[50]
- It eliminates School Breakfast start-up and expansion grants and makes funding for the Nutrition Education and Training (NET) program optional for each state.
- Nonexempt 18 to 50-year-olds are not eligible for food stamps for more than 3 months out of 36 unless they are working or participating in a workfare or training program.
- In determining eligibility for benefits, the vehicle allowance is determined by the states.[51]
- PRWORA gave states the right to issue one-year residency requirements so that poor people would not be tempted to move into their state, but the Supreme Court deemed this unconstitutional.[52]

RELIGIOUS LEADERS RESPOND TO PRWORA

Between Clinton's pledge and his actual signing of the PRWORA, David Saperstein of the Religious Action Center of Reform Judaism wrote:

It is not surprising that a broad coalition of religious groups—Protestant, Catholic, Evangelical, Jewish, and others—have raised their voices together in opposition to this welfare legislation. . . . We all of us here this morning, have gathered to ask a simple question: how can Congress and the president possibly reconcile their support for legislative proposals, which leave more children, more disabled people, more legal immigrants in hunger and poverty, with the clear Biblical mandate to care for the most needy of God's children?[53]

By pointing to the remarkable coalition of religious leaders opposed to this bill, Rabbi Saperstein, among others, wanted to know why their voices were not being heard.

Cardinal Roger Mahoney accused the federal government of "reneging on its responsibilities."[54] He also claimed, "Workfare should not be an opportunity for employers to cut labor costs by displacing current employees with workfare participants paid at lower wages."

The United Methodist General Conference issued the statement, "An acceptable welfare program must result in lifting people out of poverty, not merely in reducing welfare roles."[55]

The General Assembly of the Presbyterian Church, U.S.A., adopted a "Resolution on Welfare and Poverty" that called on the federal government "to invest in job creation programs that result in employment at livable wages, beyond what is provided for in the 1996 legislation, restore $27 billion cut from the food stamp program, and maintain funding of the Temporary Assistance to Needy Families block grants to the states beyond 2002."[56]

Jesse Jackson, disappointed that Bill Clinton had vowed to support the PRWORA, claimed that the government was removing the ceiling for the rich and the floor from the poor. He argued that the message was clear, the rich can get richer "and the poor can go to hell."[57] Anticipating the argument that African Americans should turn their backs on the Democratic Party, however, Jackson warned, "not to vote is to vote for Dole and Gingrich."[58] Defending the "realism" of his position, Jackson would claim, "We are mature enough to differ without splitting. . . . That's what makes democracy real."[59]

In contrast to Jackson's realism, Hans Holznagel of the United Church Board for Homeland Ministries reflected the attitude of many white, Mainline Protestant leaders, "Religious and moral arguments will probably not change the dominant values. . . . We are up against funding, unanimity, one political party and part of another."[60] Concurring with Holznagel, Arthur Cribbs, Jr., executive director for the United Church of Christ Office of Communication, points to the solution. "We need a strategy of newsroom advocacy. . . . We need to lobby on the inside."[61]

CONCLUSIONS

The religious far Left has become its own caricature by denying that individual choices ever lead to poverty, by ignoring the legitimate concerns of the American people, and by demanding perfect justice while otherwise accepting the status quo. They are unwilling to imagine new solutions to the very real problem of poverty in America. They seem unwilling to consider the possibility that at some point the American people will receive increasingly marginal returns on their efforts to eradicate poverty through federal programs. If the American people were to uncritically embrace the proposals of the religious far Left, we might well have a society where all are equally impoverished.

The religious far Right, on the other hand, argues that the federal government is not responsible for ensuring the well-being of its poorest citizens, that such "Marxist" programs had been imposed on American society by secular elites, and that *laissez faire* capitalism is the Christian alternative. Refusing to allow history to stand in the way of ideology, they advocate policies that harken back to the good old days of the nineteenth-century robber barons. In the context of the Great Depression, Americans of all religious denominations and both political parties had united in proclaiming, "Never again!" Perhaps one generation is all it takes to lose such a lesson. If the American people were to uncritically embrace the proposals of the religious far Right, we might well have a society where a handful of people live as kings while the masses live in poverty.

NOTES

1. Christian Coalition, *Contract with the American Family: A Bold Plan by the Christian Coalition to Strengthen the Family and Restore Common-Sense Values* (Nashville: Moorings, 1995), 86.

2. Ed Gillespie and Bob Schellhas, eds., *Contract with America: The Bold Plan by Rep. Newt Gingrich, Rep. Dick Armey and the House Republicans to Change the Nation* (New York: Times Books, 1994), 65.

3. Ibid., 75. This element of their pledge would be rejected by the more moderate Republicans in the Senate. See Elizabeth Shogren, "Senate, House on Own Paths in Welfare Debate," *Los Angeles Times* (16 September 1995), A4. According to Shogren, "By rejecting provisions intended to discourage single women from having babies, the Senate put the Christian Coalition and similar grass-roots groups on notice that it disapproves of the House's proclivity to mandate family values through legislation."

4. Ibid., 66.

5. Ibid., 66.

6. Ibid., 67. For an alternative view of the War on Poverty, see John E. Schwarz, *America's Hidden Success: A Reassessment of Twenty Years of Public Policy* (New York: W. W. Norton, 1983), 79–114.

7. *Contract with America*, 67.

8. Ibid., 73.

9. Ibid., 21.

10. Don Feder, "Smash the Welfare Culture: The Left Is No Stranger to Hate," *The Boston Herald* (28 November 1994), 23. Feder has been a columnist for the

Boston Herald since 1983. He is also the author of *Who's Afraid of the Religious Right* and *A Jewish Conservative Looks at Pagan America.* He has addressed national conventions for the Christian Coalition, Concerned Women for America, College Republicans, and the Heritage Foundation.

11. Ibid.

12. Marvin Olasky, *Renewing American Compassion* (New York: Free Press, 1996), 32.

13. Ibid., 170.

14. Ibid., 173.

15. Ibid., 176.

16. Ibid., 180.

17. Ibid., 168.

18. "GOP Welfare Plan Draws Criticism," *St. Petersburg Times* (11 March 1995), City Times, Briefly, Religion, 10.

19. Tom Rhodes, "Church Fights U.S. Child Benefit Cuts," *The Times* (20 March 1995), Overseas News.

20. "Excerpts from Statement by Bishops," *The New York Times* (19 March 1995), 1:26. The full statement is also published in *Origins* 24, no. 41 (30 March 1995), 673–77.

21. Darrell Holland, "Pilla Finds 'Meanness' in Welfare Reform Debate," *The Plain Dealer,* (30 March 1995), 2B. For an analysis of the various types of action taken by the U.S. Catholic Bishops during the welfare reform debates, see Thomas Massaro, *Catholic Social Teaching and United States Welfare Reform* (Collegeville, Minn.: Liturgical Press, 1998), 133–49.

22. Darrell Holland, "Bishops Conference Encouraged to Take New Stand for the Poor," *The Plain Dealer* (14 November 1995), 1B.

23. Ibid.

24. Associated Press, "Catholic Bishops Refuse to Bend Principles for Politics," *Los Angeles Times,* (5 November 1995), A24.

25. Ibid. For an elaboration of the Catholic bishops' critique of the Christian Coalition's Catholic Alliance, see Ben Winton, "Coalition Effort Worries Bishops: Pat Robertson Group Targets Catholics, Offers Politics at Odds with Church," *The Arizona Republic* (31 December 1995), A1.

26. "UCC on Welfare Reform," *The Plain Dealer* (10 December 1994), 7E. For more detailed accounts of the extent of welfare fraud in relation to the stereotype of the "welfare queen who drives a Cadillac," see the United States Department of Labor, *About Welfare: Myths, Facts, Challenges and Solutions* (Washington, D.C.: U.S. G.P.O., 1997); Karen Seccombe, *So You Think I Drive a Cadillac? Welfare Recipients' Perspectives on the System and Its Reform* (Boston: Allyn and Bacon, 1999); David Zucchino, *Myth of the Welfare Queen* (New York: Scribner, 1997).

27. Thomas Hart, "Welfare Reform: April 4, 1995," Episcopal Public Policy Network, URL: http://www.ecusa.anglican.org/eppn/WELF495.HTML (accessed 29 October 1998), 1. Also see action alerts on 19 June 1995, 11 October 1995, and 15 July 1996.

28. Ibid. Also see action alerts on 19 June 1995, 11 October 1995, and 15 July 1996.

29. Division for Church in Society of the Evangelical Lutheran Church in America, *Give Us This Day Our Daily Bread: Sufficient, Sustainable, Livelihood for All* (Chicago: Division of Church in Society, ELCA, 1996), 39.

30. Ibid., 39–44.

31. Ibid., 67.

32. Ibid.

33. Ibid.

34. Ibid., 68.

35. Ibid.

36. Carol J. Fouke, "Statement on Welfare Reform Legislation by the Rev. Dr. Joan Brown Campbell, General Secretary, National Council of the Churches of Christ in the U.S.A," *Worldwide Faith News Archive* (18 July 1996), URL: http://www.wfn.org/conferences/wfn.news/199607/1756118821.html (accessed 1 October 1999), 2.

37. Charles W. Rawlings and Janet Parker, eds., *Advocating Justice and Equity: A Policy Resource Guide on Welfare, Work and Economic Policy* (Elkhart, Ind. Economic Justice and Domestic Hunger Program Ministry of the National Council of Churches, 1998), front cover.

38. United Synagogue of Conservative Judaism, *Position Papers: Welfare Reform* (26 January 1995), URL: http://www.uscj.org/scripts/uscj/paper/Article.asp?ArticleID=24 (accessed 11 December 1998), 1.

39. Ibid.

40. David Saperstein, "News Conference of Religious and Charitable Leaders on Welfare Reform" (Washington, D.C.: Religious Action Center of Reform Judaism, 18 July 1996), URL: http://www.rj.org/rac/news/wlflrds.html (accessed 3 October 1999), 1.

41. Ibid.

42. Elizabeth Shogren, "Religious Groups Attack GOP Welfare, Medicaid Plans," *Los Angeles Times* (9 November 1995), A35. The article also goes on to point out, "The Christian Coalition and conservative Christian groups, for example, have heartily supported the Republican welfare reform effort and favor the tougher House version over the somewhat milder Senate plan."

43. After promising to "end welfare as we know it," Bill Clinton had already vetoed two welfare reform bills. Public opinion polls showed strong support for the plan. (For example, 71 percent of Gallup Poll interviewees supported efforts to cut welfare benefits to people who had not become self-sufficient after two years. Such opinions contrast sharply with the 75 percent who favored maintaining or increasing welfare spending in 1972.) With the 1996 elections coming and a vivid memory of the Republican landslide in 1994, Clinton's decision to support this policy can be interpreted either as opportunistic or as prudent. Responding to Clinton's decision to support PRWORA, Republican presidential candidate Bob Dole claimed, "There's not a dime's worth of difference between the bill he talked about today and the one he vetoed a few months back. . . . The only difference is it's 97 days before the election." See Douglas Turner, "House Passes GOP Welfare-Overhaul Bill as Clinton Agrees to Sign It," *The Buffalo News* (1 August 1996), 1A.

44. U.S. Department of Health and Human Services, "HHS Fact Sheet: Clinton Administration Finalizes Welfare Regulations" (9 April 1999), URL: http://www.acf.dhhs.gov/news/3tanfreg.htm (accessed 31 August 1999), 1.

45. U.S. Department of Health and Human Services, "Comparison of Prior Law and the Personal Responsibility and Work Opportunity Reconciliation Act of 1996

(P.L. 104–193)," URL: http://aspe.os.dhhs.gov/hsp/isp/reform.htm (accessed 31 August 1999), 5.

46. In fiscal year 1996, Congress appropriated $954 million to the states to help parents pay for child care. U.S. Congress, Senate, Report to the Ranking Minority Member, Subcommittee on Children and Families, Committee on Labor and Human Resources, *Welfare Reform: Implications of Increased Work Participation for Child Care* GAO/HEHS-97-75 (Washington, D.C.: United States General Accounting Office, June 1998), 3.

47. "Comparison of Prior Law and the PRWORA", 2. For example, my own state of Indiana has set the limit at two years for adults. See U.S. Department of Health and Human Services, "Time Provisions of State TANF Plans," URL: http://www.acf.dhhs.gov/programs/ofa/TIME2.HTM (accessed 31 August 1999), 4.

48. This rule does not apply for convictions that occurred before this law was enacted.

49. Exemptions are made for refugees and dependents of Armed Forces personnel.

50. Critics of the old system argued that welfare benefits served as an incentive for poor people from other nations to immigrate illegally into the United States. In 1996, there were roughly five million illegal aliens in the United States. A child who is born in the United States, regardless of the citizenship of her parents, is considered an American citizen. "In fiscal year 1995, about $1.1 billion in AFDC and food stamp benefits were provided to households with an illegal alien parent for the use of his or her citizen child. This amount accounted for about 3 percent of AFDC and 2 percent of food stamp benefit costs." U.S. Congress, Senate, Committee on the Judiciary of the United States Senate, *Illegal Aliens: Extent of Welfare Benefits Received on Behalf of U.S. Citizen Children,* GA 1.13:HEHS-98-30 (Washington D.C.: United States General Accounting Office, 1997), 3.

51. In my own state of Indiana, legislators chose to set the vehicle allowance at $1000. See U.S. Department of Health and Human Services, "Asset Provisions of State TANF Plans," URL: http://www.acf.dhhs.gov/programs/ofa/ASSET2.HTM (accessed August 31, 1999), 2. Indiana legislators feel that $1000 automobiles are sufficient, in part, because Indiana's public transportation system boasts "820 public transit, specialized, taxi, school bus and intercity transportation providers operating a total 4,301 vehicles." U.S. Department of Health and Human Services, "Transportation in Welfare Reform" (June 1999), URL:http://www.acf.dhhs.gov/programs/ofa/TRANS2.HTM (accessed 31 August 1999), 5.

52. Supreme Court of the United States, "Rita L. Saenz, Director, California Department of Social Services, et al., Petitioners v. Brenda Roe and Anna Doe, etc.," No. 98-97 (17 May 1999), 16. The Majority opinion claimed that the Fourteenth Amendment "does not provide for, and does not allow for, degrees of citizenship based on length of residence." They further argued that "Neither the duration of respondents' California residence, nor the identity of their prior States of residence, has any relevance to their need for benefits," 17. Quoting their decision in *Shapiro v. Thompson,* they claimed, "Appellants' reasoning would logically permit the State to bar new residents from schools, parks, and libraries or deprive them of police and fire protection. Indeed it would permit the State to apportion all benefits and services according to the past tax contributions of citizens," 17.

The Supreme Court concluded that "Citizens of the United States, whether rich or poor, have the right to choose to be citizens 'of the state wherein they reside.' . . . The States, however, do not have any right to select their citizens," 21. It is worth noting, however, that Chief Justice Rehnquist's dissent points to the precedent of one-year residency requirements in the cases of in-state tuition rates at state universities, divorce laws, and political party registrations (7–8).

53. David Saperstein, "National Leaders Speak Out on Welfare Reform" (Washington D.C.: Religious Action Center of Reform Judaism, 29 July 1996), URL: http://www.rj.org/rac/news/wlf2rds.html (accessed 3 October 1999), 1.

54. Patrick J. McDonnell, "Mahony Says Poor Need a 'Safety Net,' " *Los Angeles Times* (30 May 1997), B1.

55. Linda Bloom, "Focus of Welfare Reform," *United Methodist Daily News* (19 February 1997), URL: http://www.wfn.org/conferences/wfn.news/199702/158433.45 (accessed 1 October 1999), 2.

56. Nancy Rodman, "Assembly Responds to Welfare Reform," *Worldwide Faith News Archives* (20 June 1997), URL: http://www.wfn.org/conferences/wfn.news/199706/1350531696.html (accessed 1 October 1999), 1.

57. Helen T. Gray, "Compassion Should Rule: Jackson Says," *The Kansas City Star* (9 August 1999), C1.

58. Ibid.

59. Catherine Candisky and Roger K. Lowe, "Jackson Backs Clinton Despite Welfare Clash," *The Columbus Dispatch* (28 August 1996), 6A.

60. Carol Fouke, "NCCCUSA Kicks Off Welfare Reform Strategy," *Worldwide Faith News Archives* (October 9, 1998), URL: http://www.wfn.org/conferences/wfn.news/199810/1768595957.html (accessed 1 July 1999), 2.

61. Ibid.

Conclusions

The culture wars thesis is among the most helpful and the most problematic conceptual tools for understanding the role of religious communities in American public policy debates in the last quarter of the twentieth century. James Hunter portrays an arguably cosmic battle between (1) an "orthodoxy of ecumenism" that consists of *conservative* Evangelicals, Catholics, Mainline Protestants, and Jews, and (2) a "progressive coalition" that consists of *liberal* atheists, Jews, Mainline Protestants, Catholics, and Evangelicals. With respect to political economy, the orthodox are said to lean toward *laissez faire* capitalism while the apostates lean toward socialism. When complemented by the elite secularization thesis of Weigel, Neuhaus, and others, one gets the impression that secular elites in education, government, the media, and liberal religious institutions have imposed a Marxist welfare state upon an unsuspecting American people. Yet, I would contend that such arguments are not merely social scientific constructs for understanding contemporary America; they are weapons used by cultural warriors in the religious right to silence the voices of secular conservatives and religious liberals. A more nuanced historical analysis demonstrates that religious leaders have played a significant role in creating and legitimating America's mixed economy, that the varieties of secularization are as potentially diverse as the varieties of religion, and that secular Americans are more likely to be rugged individualists than socialists.

At America's birth, the philosophy of *laissez faire* capitalism was hardly contested. The U.S. economic policies, or lack thereof, seemed to be predicated upon the assumption that the free market would distribute goods and services efficiently and equitably. With the industrial age, however, economic relations were transformed. Exchanges between employers and employees, producers and consumers, creditors and borrowers became more anonymous and impersonal. The illusion of America's endless supply of capital would diminish along with its Western frontier. The creation of factories of mass production would increase the productivity of workers, the profit rates for those who owned the means of production, and the buying power of consumers. Yet, it also increased the ability of those who owned the means of production to exploit laborers. As the owners of the means of production found new ways to reduce the skill necessary to produce their goods, individual laborers became increasingly expendable.

In the midst of immense toil and suffering, "robber barons" accumulated wealth beyond which human beings had hitherto thought impossible.[1] More scrupulous capitalists who sought to pay their workers a just wage were often put out of business by less scrupulous capitalists in cooperation with consumers who could not or would not consider the processes of production in selecting their products. A large supply of unemployed and unpropertied laborers ensured that wages could be kept low. Being bound to no conception of a higher good, unscrupulous capitalists would pit laborer against laborer in one community and then another to maximize their profits. The "invisible hand" of capitalism seemed not only invisible, but also illusory to a growing number of Americans.

America's most renowned defender of fundamentalism, William Jennings Bryan, has provided some of the most profound critiques of the Social Darwinism inherent in the libertarian justifications for *laissez faire* capitalism. Allowing the poor and the weak to perish seemed inimical to Bryan's evangelical faith. Since private charity proved no match for the market failures of unbridled capitalism, Bryan, the three-time U.S. presidential candidate, advocated a platform for which he is sometimes called *the father of the modern Democratic Party*. He was soundly defeated, in part, because most voters rejected his *liberal* views on political economy at the time.

Leaders in the American Catholic Church were also on the forefront in challenging the *laissez faire* theories that dominated American public policy debates. Encouraged by Pope Leo's *Rerum Novarum,* the U.S. Catholic Bishops joined John Ryan in articulating the "Program of Social Reconstruction." At the dawn of the twentieth century, the "orthodox" view of Catholic social teaching became increasingly identified with a "mixed economy" that rejects the false promises of *laissez faire* capitalism and communism.

Meanwhile, an influential group of Jewish leaders and Mainline Protestants in the Social Gospel tradition also articulated the view that government should play a role in meeting the needs of society's most vulnerable members. These religious leaders were a small but vocal minority whose time had not yet come. Their critiques of unbridled capitalism were certainly not the dominant view during the "roaring twenties." It was still possible for the majority of voters to believe that America, the land of opportunity, allowed anybody to succeed if only they would pull themselves up by the bootstraps.

The Great Depression, however, burst this idealistic vision of *laissez faire* capitalism. It was no longer possible for most Americans to simply blame the poor for their own poverty. Religious leaders across the theological spectrum played an instrumental role in justifying the type of New Deal legislation initiated by Franklin D. Roosevelt. The state, which had played no small role in defending the propertied class, increasingly adopted policies of regulating industry, defending a limited right for workers to organize labor unions, and providing a safety net to those who had been unable to sell their labor in exchange for a living wage. Implementation of these New Deal programs corresponded with a remarkable shift in public opinion about government responsibility for the well-being of its citizens.

Throughout most of the twentieth century, liberal economic theories prevailed.[2] Not only did Americans continue to support New Deal legislation, three Republican and five Democratic presidents (to varying degrees) contributed to America's welfare state. Nevertheless, American public policy debates on economic issues would, at times, be influenced by the Cold War. While some Americans would conceptualize the Cold War as a battle between Christian capitalism and atheistic communism, the vital center of U.S. public policy was more indebted to the U.S. Catholic Bishops and Mainline Protestant leaders such as Reinhold Niebuhr whose liberal anti-communism would advocate a U.S. foreign policy of containing communism while simultaneously supporting a domestic policy of escalating America's war on poverty. By the late 1970s, however the American public had grown increasingly cautious about what appeared to be an ever-expanding welfare system.

The rise of the New Christian Right can be understood, in part, as a reaction by conservative Christians to what they describe as the unambiguous endorsement of the Democratic Party by Mainline Protestant, Catholic, and Jewish leaders. While conservative views toward the Bible continue to correspond with liberal views on poverty, the introduction of Christian Social Darwinism appears to be having some effect upon how evangelical leaders conceptualize poverty. As a result of this reconceptualization, organizations like the Christian Coalition were among the most vocal opponents of the Health Security Act (that sought to guarantee universal access to health care for all Americans) and among the most ardent supporters of the Personal Responsibility and Work Opportunity Reconciliation Act (that eliminated the federal guarantee of a safety net for poor Americans with children). The five fallacies of wartime logic provide further insights into the tragedy that some contemporary Evangelicals have inverted Bryan's populist movement in order to advocate a philosophy of rugged individualism that demonstrates no compassion for society's most vulnerable members. First, cultural war-riors in the evangelical camp assume that if Right is good, further Right is better. Second, they present false dichotomies: either you are for Christian capitalism or you are for atheistic communism. They reject the welfare state as a watered-down version of communism. Third, assuming that "the enemy of my enemy must be my friend," they embrace the ideas of Darwin and Nietzsche to avoid the atheism of Karl Marx. Fourth, they believe that humiliating "the enemy" is a necessary prerequisite for a lasting peace—as their responses to President Clinton's impeachment trial might well attest. Fifth, they conclude that if our side cannot win the war, we must poison the wells so that nobody wins. Therefore, the politics of personal destruction permeate the public square.

Cultural warriors in the Mainline Protestant camp, however, have not fared much better. While Mainline Protestants continue to advocate mod-erate views on public policy and lean slightly toward the Republican Party, their leaders often advocate policies left of the Democratic Party. For exam-ple, they disregarded Bill Clinton's Health Security Act and advocated a single-payer system. The five fallacies of wartime logic provide insights into the absurdity that some Mainline Protestant leaders have inverted Niebuhr's realism to lobby on behalf of policies that their own constituents would not even accept. First, cultural warriors in the Protestant mainline assume that if Left is good, further to the left is better. Second, they present false dichotomies: either you are prophetic or you are relevant. Therefore, they have become the religious community most likely to demand perfect justice while otherwise accepting the status quo. Third, assuming that "the enemy of my enemy must be my friend," they naïvely conclude that all opponents of the New Christian Right must be their allies. Fourth, believ-ing that humiliating the enemy is a necessary prerequisite for a lasting peace, they have contributed to the character assassinations of figures like Jim Bakker, Tammy Bakker, and Pat Robertson. Fifth, they conclude that if our side cannot win the war, we must poison the wells so that nobody wins. In the process of divorcing ends from means, they often mirror what they claim to dislike about the New Christian Right.

The National Conference of Catholic Bishops is often more representa-tive of its constituents than its Protestant counterparts. When Protestants do not like resolutions adopted by their denominational or ecumenical lead-ers, they form a new denomination or they ignore the ecumenical bodies that claim to speak on their behalf. The sharp division between the Protes-tant Left and the Protestant Right in the contemporary culture wars is largely a result of this continued process. By way of contrast, Catholic lead-ers tend to work out their differences or remain in a constructive tension with the institution; thus, Catholic resolutions tend to be more balanced than resolutions adopted by Protestant denominations and their ecumenical bodies. The National Conference of Catholic Bishops is uniquely situated to mediate the culture wars, to find the common ground beyond the inflammatory rhetoric, and to shape the new vital center for U.S. public policy debates, that is, if they can avoid the temptation to reduce their social teachings to the single issue of abortion. Far from tragic or absurd, this new role is, nevertheless, ironic for a Catholic community that has perceived itself as an embattled minority throughout much of U.S. history.

While I have focused upon health care reform and welfare reform, America's religious communities have also responded in predictable ways to economic policy debates on issues such as the Social Security crisis, the budget deficit, the reassessment of tax rates, charitable choice legislation, Third World debt relief, campaign finance reform, environmental protection policies, and many more. Those on the Left in the culture wars fear that if the Christian Coalition and other such organizations succeed in shaping public perceptions of religion, then religion will be perceived as a tool for the powerful to justify the oppression of the poor. Those on the Right in the culture wars assume that they are fighting in a nearly cosmic battle against secular elites in education, the media, and even liberal religious communities.

Nevertheless, the greatest threat to the credibility of religion in the modern world comes not from secular elites; it comes from the religious communities themselves. Inasmuch as religious leaders become cultural warriors for narrow political agendas, they feed the perception that religion is merely adornment for self-interested politics. The New Christian Right fulfills the expectations of those, like Marx, who contend that religion is an oppressive force in human history. Many Mainline Protestant leaders, on the other hand, fulfill the expectations of those, like Nietzsche, who contend that religion is mere sentimentality.[3] Inasmuch as religious people remove themselves from the "corrupt world of politics," however, they exacerbate the fears of those, like Elie Wiesel suffering in the concentration camps during the Holocaust,[4] who ask, "Where is God?"

NOTES

1. Charles Dickens provides dramatic illustrations of the exploitation associated with nineteenth-century capitalism through such novels as *A Christmas Carol, A Tale of Two Cities, Great Expectations, The Adventures of Oliver Twist,* and *Hard Times.* In a different genre, a recent United Nations Human Development Report provides a statistical analysis of the injustices of the contemporary economic order by pointing out that the United States has the highest average income and the highest poverty rates among the industrialized nations. Drawing attention to global inequalities, the report claims that the richest fifth of the world's population consumes 86 percent of all private goods while the poorest fifth consumes only 1.3 percent. Emphasizing the gap between rich and poor, they show that the world's richest 225 people (60 of whom are Americans) have a combined wealth equal to the annual income of the poorest 47 percent of the world's population. Placing the wealth of the richest 225 people into a global perspective, the report claims that less

than 4 percent of their combined wealth would be required to fund basic education, adequate food, safe water, and healthy sanitation for all the world's impoverished people. United Nations Development Programme, *Human Development Report 1998* (New York: Oxford University Press, 1998), 28, 2, 30.

2. Liberalism here is understood as a pragmatic political philosophy that lies between the philosophies of libertarianism and socialism, between the demands for perfect freedom and for perfect justice, and between individualism and collectivism.

3. If the critics of religion like Marx and Nietzsche have correctly identified some of the potential dangers of religion, their followers have demonstrated the potential dangers of "secularization."

4. See Elie Wiesel, *The Night Trilogy* (New York: Noonday Press, 1988; reprint, 1972), 38–54.

Selected Bibliography

Abbott, Walter M., ed. *The Documents of Vatican II*. New York: Guild, 1966.

Allitt, Patrick. *Catholic Intellectuals and Conservative Politics in America: 1950–1985*. Ithaca, N.Y.: Cornell University Press, 1993.

Anderson, David E. "Council Stands on Health Care." *Petersburg Times* (20 November 1993), 5.

Associated Press. "Catholic Bishops Refuse to Bend Principles for Politics." *Los Angeles Times* (5 November 1995), A24.

Banfield, Edward. *The Unheavenly City Revisited*. Boston: Little, Brown & Co. 1974.

Benson, Peter, and Dorothy Williams. *Religion on Capitol Hill: Myths and Realities*. New York: Oxford University Press, 1982.

Billingsley, K. L. *From Mainline to Sideline: The Social Witness of the National Council of Churches*. Washington, D.C.: Ethics and Public Policy Center, 1990.

Bolce, Louis, and Gerald De Maio. "Religious Outlook, Culture War Politics, and Antipathy toward Christian Fundamentalists." *Public Opinion Quarterly* 63 (spring 1999), 29–31.

Browne, Henry J. *The Catholic Church and the Knights of Labor*. Washington, D.C.: University of America Press, 1949.

Bryan, William Jennings, and Mary Baird Bryan. *The Memoirs of William Jennings Bryan*. Chicago: John C. Winston Company, 1925.

Budde, Michael. *The (Magic) Kingdom of God: Christianity and Global Culture Industries*. Boulder: Westview Press, 1997.

Byrnes, Timothy A. *Catholic Bishops in American Politics*. Princeton: Princeton University Press, 1991.

Carter, Jimmy. "Can Religious Faith Promote Peace?" in *Theology, Politics, and Peace*. Ed. Theodore Runyon. Maryknoll, N.Y.: Orbis Books, 1989.

Carter, Stephen. *The Culture of Disbelief: How American Law and Politics Trivialize Religious Devotion.* New York: Anchor, 1994; reprint, New York: Basic Books, 1993.

Cherry, Conrad. *Hurrying toward Zion: Universities, Divinity Schools, and American Protestantism.* Bloomington, Ind.: Indiana University Press, 1995.

Chilton, David. *Productive Christians in an Age of Guilt-Manipulators: A Biblical Response to Ronald J. Sider.* Tyler, Tex.: Institute for Christian Economics, 1981.

Christian Coalition. *Contract with the American Family: A Bold Plan by the Christian Coalition to Strengthen the Family and Restore Common-Sense Values.* Nashville: Moorings, 1995.

Chupp, Nancy. "Health Care Access Campaign." *Christian Social Action* 4 (February 1993).

Clinton, William J. *Weekly Compilation of Presidential Documents* 29–30, 1993–1994.

Clydesdale, Timothy T. "Toward Understanding the Role of Bible Beliefs and Higher Education in American Attitudes toward Eradicating Poverty, 1964–1996." *The Journal for the Scientific Study of Religion* 38 (March 1999), 103.

Cohen, Naomi W. "Between Left and Right." In *The American Jewish Committee: 1906–1966.* Philadelphia: Jewish Publication Society of America, 1972, 345–82.

Cohen, Steven M. *American Modernity and Jewish Identity.* New York: Travistock, 1983.

Coletta, Paolo E. *William Jennings Bryan: III, Political Puritan (1915–1925).* Lincoln: University of Nebraska Press, 1969.

Coomaraswamy, Ananda. "What Has India Contributed to Human Welfare," In *The Dance of Shiva.* New York: Dover Publication, 1985; New York: Sunwise Turn, 1924, 2–17.

Cooney, John. *The American Pope: The Life and Times of Francis Cardinal Spellman.* New York: Times Books, 1984.

Curran, Charles E. "John A. Ryan." In *American Catholic Social Ethics: Twentieth Century Approaches.* Notre Dame: University of Notre Dame Press, 1982.

Curran, R. Emmett. "Confronting 'The Social Question': American Catholic Thought and the Socio-Economic Order in the Nineteenth Century." *U.S. Catholic Historian* 5 (1986), 165–94.

Dart, John. "Groups Debate Clinton Health Care Plan; Politics: Christian Coalition in Studio City Calls Proposal Anti-Family. Clergy Network Luncheon in Reseda Says 'Everybody Should Be Covered.' " *Los Angeles Times* (26 March 1994), B:11.

Darwin, Charles. *The Descent of Man, and Selection in Relation to Sex.* Introduction by John Tyler Bonner and Robert M. May. Princeton, N.J.: Princeton University Press, 1981.

Darwin, Francis. *The Life and Letters of Charles Darwin: I.* New York: P. F. Collier & Son, 1888.

Decker, Cathleen. "Clinton Details His Plan for Welfare Reform." *Los Angeles Times* (10 September 1992), A1.

Division for Church in Society of the Evangelical Lutheran Church in America. *Give Us This Day Our Daily Bread: Sufficient, Sustainable, Livelihood for All.* Chicago: Division of Church in Society, ELCA, 1996.

Dobson, James C. *Straight Talk to Men and Their Wives*. Dallas: Word Publishing, 1991.

Doran, Kevin P. *Solidarity: A Synthesis of Personalism and Communalism in the Thought of Karol Wojtyla/Pope John Paul II*. New York: Peter Lang, 1996.

Dorr, Donald. *Option for the Poor: A Hundred Years of Vatican Social Teaching*. Maryknoll, N.Y.: Orbis Books, 1983.

Dorrien, Gary. *Soul in Society: The Making and Renewal of Social Christianity*. Minneapolis: Fortress Press, 1995.

Eidsmore, John. *God and Caesar: Biblical Faith and Political Action*. Westchester, Ill.: Crossways Books, 1984.

Einstein, Albert. "Science and Religion." In *Out of My Later Years*. Totowa, N.J.: Littlefield, Adams, 1967; Philosophical Library, 1950.

Ellis, John Tracy. *The Life of James Cardinal Gibbons: Archbishop of Baltimore, 1834–1921*. Milwaukee: Bruce, 1952.

Esposito, John L. *Islam: The Straight Path*. New York: Oxford University Press, 1988.

Falwell, Jerry. *Listen America*. New York: Bantam Books, 1981; Doubleday, 1980.

Feder, Don. "Smash the Welfare Culture: The Left Is No Stranger to Hate." *The Boston Herald* (28 November 1994), 23.

Feurbach, Ludwig. *The Essence of Christianity*. Trans. George Eliot. New York: Harper & Row, 1957.

Finn, James, ed. *Global Economics and Religion*. New Brunswick: Transaction Books, 1983.

Fowler, Robert Booth, and Allen D. Hertzke. *Religion and Politics in America: Faith, Culture, and Strategic Choices*. Boulder: Westview, 1995.

French, Marilyn. *The War Against Women*. New York: Summit Books, 1992.

Freud, Sigmund. *The Future of an Illusion*. Trans. W. D. Robson-Scott. New York: Liveright Publishing, 1953.

Friedman, Milton, and Rose Friedman. *Free to Choose*. New York: Harcourt, Brace, Jovanovich, 1980.

Fuchs, Lawrence H. *John F. Kennedy and American Catholicism*. New York: Meredith, 1967.

Fuchs, Lawrence H. *The Political Behavior of American Jews*. Glencoe, Ill.: Free Press, 1956.

Fuechtmann, Thomas G., ed. *Consistent Ethic of Life: Joseph Cardinal Bernardin*. Kansas City, Mo: Sheed & Ward, 1988.

Galeano, Eduardo. *Open Veins of Latin America: Five Centuries of the Pillage of a Continent*. Trans. Cedric Belfrage. New York: Monthly Review Press, 1973.

Gandhi, Mohandas, K. *An Autobiography: The Story of My Experiments with Truth*. Boston: Beacon Press, 1957.

Gannon, Thomas F., ed. *The Catholic Challenge to the American Economy: Reflections on the U.S. Bishops' Pastoral Letter on Catholic Social Teaching and the U.S. Economy*. New York: Macmillan Publishing Company, 1987.

Gilder, George. *Sexual Suicide*. New York: Quadrangle/New York Times Book Co., 1973.

Gilder, George. *Wealth and Poverty*. New York: Basic Books, 1981.

Gillespie, Ed, and Bob Schellhas, eds. *Contract with America: The Bold Plan by Rep. Newt Gingrich, Rep. Dick Armey and the House Republicans to Change the Nation*. New York: Times Books, 1994.

Gossett, Thomas F. *Race: The History of an Idea in America.* New York: Schocken Books, 1963.

Gottfried, Robert R. *Economics, Ecology, and the Roots of Western Faith.* Lanham, Md.: Rowman & Littlefield, 1995.

Grant, George. *Bringing in the Sheaves: Transforming Poverty into Productivity.* Brentwood, Tenn.: Wolgemuch & Hyatt, 1988.

Grant, George Parkin. *In the Shadow of Plenty: The Biblical Blueprint for Welfare.* Ft. Worth, Tex.: Dominion Press; Nashville, Tenn.: Thomas Nelson, 1986.

Gray, Helen T. "Compassion Should Rule: Jackson Says." *The Kansas City Star.* (9 August 1999), C1.

Green, John. "Religion, Social Issues, and the Christian Right." In *Disciplines and Democracy: Religious Conservatives and the Future of American Politics.* Ed. Michael Cromartie. Grand Rapids: Eerdmans, 1994.

Guth, James L., and John C. Green. "God's Own Party: Evangelicals and Republicans in the '92 Election." *Christian Century* 110, no. 5 (17 February 1993), 172.

Guth, James L., John C. Green, Corwin E. Smidt, Lyman A. Kellstedt, and Margaret M. Poloma. *The Bully Pulpit: The Politics of Protestant Clergy.* Lawrence: University Press of Kansas, 1997.

Gutierrez, Gustavo. *A Theology of Liberation: History, Politics and Salvation.* Ed. and trans. Caridad Inda and John Eagleson. Maryknoll, N.Y.: Orbis Books, 1973.

Hadden, Jeffrey K. *The Gathering Storm in the Churches.* New York: Doubleday, 1969.

Hadden, Jeffrey K., and Anson Shupe, eds. *Religion and the Political Order,* vol. 3, *Secularization and Fundamentalism Reconsidered.* New York: Paragon, 1989.

Haines, Byron L. "Perspectives of American Churches on Islam and the Muslim Community in America: An Analysis of Some Official and Unofficial Statements." In *The Muslims of America.* Ed. Yvonne Y. Haddad. New York: Oxford University Press, 1991.

Hamilton, Clarence H. *Buddhism: A Religion of Infinite Compassion.* New York: Liberal Arts Press, 1954; reprint 1952.

Hammond, Phillip E., ed. *The Sacred in a Secular Age: Toward Revision in the Scientific Study of Religion.* Berkeley: University of California Press, 1985.

Harvey, Van. *Feurbach and the Interpretation of Religion.* Cambridge Studies in Religion and Critical Thought I. Cambridge: Cambridge University Press, 1995.

Henderson, Hazel. "The Love Economy: Toward Sustainable Human Development." *SGI Quarterly: Buddhist Perspectives on Peace, Culture and Education* (October 1998), 3–7.

Herberg, Will. *Protestant, Catholic, Jew: An Essay in American Religious Sociology.* Garden City, N.Y.: Doubleday, 1955.

Herrnstein, Richard J., and Charles Murray. *The Bell Curve: Intelligence and Class Structure in American Life.* New York: Free Press, 1994.

Hobbes, Thomas. *Leviathan.* Ed. C. B. Macpherson. New York: Viking Penguin, Inc., 1968.

Hofstadter, Richard. *Social Darwinism in American Thought.* New York: George Braziller, Inc., 1959.

Holland, Darrell. "Religious Leaders Support Health Reform; Pat Robertson's Opposition Campaign Draws Criticism." *Plain Dealer* (9 April 1994), 8F.

Hosler, Karen. "Abortion Issue Threatens to Torpedo Health Reform." *Baltimore Sun* (14 July 1994), 1A.

Hunter, James Davison. *Culture Wars: The Struggle to Define America.* New York: Basic Books, 1991.

Interreligious Health Care Access Campaign. *Working Principles for Assessing National Health Care Legislation.* Washington, D.C.: Author, 1992.

Ireland, John. *The Church and Modern Society.* New York: D. H. McBride, 1897.

Isaacs, Stephen D. *Jews and American Politics.* New York: Doubleday & Co., 1974.

Johnson, James T., and George Weigel. "The Churches in the Gulf Crisis." *Just War and the Gulf War.* Washington, D.C.: Ethics and Public Policy Center, 1991.

Johnson, Steve A. "Political Activity of Muslims in America." In *The Muslims of America.* Ed. Yvonne Yazbeck Haddad. New York: Oxford University Press, 1991.

Kelley, Dean. *Why Conservative Churches Are Growing: A Study in Sociology of Religion.* Macon, Ga.: Mercer University Press, 1972; reprint, Macon, Ga.: Rose/Mercer University Press 1986.

Kennedy, John W. "RX for America." *Christianity Today* (25 April 1994), 40.

Keynes, John Maynard. *The General Theory of Employment, Interest, and Money.* New York: Harcourt, Brace, 1935.

King, Martin Luther, Jr. "An Address before the National Press Club." *Congressional Record* 108 (20 July 1962), 14247–49.

King, Martin Luther, Jr. "Remaining Awake through a Great Revolution." *Congressional Record* 114, no. 7 (9 April 1968), 9395–96.

King, Martin Luther, Jr. *Stride toward Freedom: The Montgomery Story.* New York: Harper & Row, 1958.

King, Martin Luther, Jr. *A Testament of Hope: The Essential Writings of Martin Luther King, Jr.* Ed. James M. Washington. San Francisco: Harper & Row, 1986.

King, Martin Luther, Jr. *Where Do We Go from Here: Chaos or Community.* New York: Harper & Row, 1967.

Kluegel, James R., and Eliot R. Smith. *Beliefs about Inequality: Americans' Views of What Is and What Ought to Be.* New York: Aldine De Gruyter, 1986.

Kroeker, P. Travis. *Christian Ethics and Political Economy in North America: A Critical Analysis.* Montreal: McGill-Queens University Press, 1995.

Kuhn, Thomas. *The Structure of Scientific Revolutions.* Chicago: University of Chicago Press, 1962.

LaHaye, Tim. *The Race for the 21st Century.* Nashville: Thomas Nelson, 1986.

LaHaye, Tim. *Sex Education Is for the Family.* Grand Rapids: Zondervan, 1985.

LaHaye, Tim. *Understanding the Male Temperament.* Old Tappan, N.J.: Fleming H. Revell Company, 1977.

Lampert, Laurence. *Nietzsche's Teaching: An Interpretation of Thus Spoke Zarathustra.* New Haven: Yale University Press, 1986.

Landsberg, Lynn F., and David Saperstein, eds. *Common Road to Justice: A Programming Manual for Blacks and Jews.* Washington, D.C.: Religious Action Center of Reform Judaism, 1991.

Liebman, Robert C., and Robert Wuthnow. *The New Christian Right: Mobilization and Legitimation.* New York: Aldine, 1983.

Lienesch, Michael. *Redeeming America: Piety and Politics in the New Christian Right.* Chapel Hill: University of North Carolina Press, 1993.

Long, Robert Emme, ed. *The Welfare Debate*. New York: H.W. Wilson, The Reference Shelf, 61, no.3, 1989.

Lovin, Robin. *Reinhold Niebuhr and Christian Realism*. New York: Cambridge University Press, 1995.

Malthus, Thomas Robert. *An Essay on the Principle of Population*. Ed. Geoffrey Gilbert. New York: Oxford University Press, 1983.

Mangum, Garth, and Bruce Blumell. *The Mormon's War on Poverty: A History of LDS Welfare, 1830–1990*. Salt Lake City: University of Utah Press, 1993.

Manza, Jeff, and Clem Brooks. "The Religious Factor in U.S. Presidential Elections, 1960–1992." *American Journal of Sociology* 103 (July 1997), 38–81.

Marx, Karl. "The Communist Manifesto." In *The Marx-Engels Reader*. Ed. Robert C. Tucker. New York: W. W. Norton, 1978, 1972.

Marx, Karl, and Friedrich Engels. *Karl Marx and Friedrich Engels on Religion*. New York: Schocken Books, 1964.

Massaro, Thomas. *Catholic Social Teaching and United States Welfare Reform*. Collegeville, Minn.: Liturgical Press, 1998.

McAvoy, Thomas. *The Great Crisis in American Catholic History: 1895–1887*. Chicago: H. Regnery Co., 1957.

McCaffrey, Lawrence J. *The Irish Diaspora in America*. Bloomington: Indiana University Press, 1976.

McDonnell, Patrick J. "Mahony Says Poor Need a 'Safety Net.'" *Los Angeles Times* (30 May 1997), B1.

Meyer, Michael A. *Response to Modernity: A History of the Reform Movement in Judaism*. New York: Oxford University Press, 1988.

Michaelsen, Robert S., and Wade Clark Roof, eds. *Liberal Protestantism: Realities and Possibilities*. New York: Pilgrim Press, 1986.

Miranda, Jose. *Marx and the Bible: A Critique of the Philosophy of Oppression*. Trans. John Eagleson. Maryknoll, N.Y.: Orbis Books, 1974.

Mollison, Andrew. "Health Care Reform: Religions Mixes with Politics in Debate over New System." *The Atlantic Journal and Constitution* (26 February 1994), C4.

Moore, David W. "Public Firm on Health Reform Goals." *The Gallup Poll Monthly* (July 1994), 12.

Mott, W. King, Jr. *The Third Way: Economic Justice According to John Paul II*. Lanham, Md.: University Press of America, 1998.

Murray, Charles. *Losing Ground: American Social Policy, 1950–1980*. New York: Basic Books, 1984.

Nanji, Azim A. "Ethics and Taxation: The Perspective of the Islamic Tradition." *The Journal of Religious Ethics* 13.1 (spring 1985), 161–77.

Nash, Ronald H. *Poverty and Wealth: The Christian Debate over Capitalism*. Westchester, Ill.: Crossways Books, 1986.

Nash, Ronald H. *Social Justice and the Christian Church*. Milford, Mich.: Mott Media, 1983.

National Conference of Catholic Bishops. *Economic Justice for All: Pastoral Letter on Catholic Social Teaching and the U.S. Economy*. Washington, D.C.: United States Catholic Conference, 1986.

National Jewish Community Relations Advisory Council. *Joint Program Plan.* New York: National Jewish Community Relations Advisory Council, 1983–84.

Neuhaus, Richard John. *The Naked Public Square: Religion and Democracy in America.* Grand Rapids: Eerdmans, 1984.

Niebuhr, H. Richard. *Christ and Culture.* New York: Harper & Row, 1951; reprint 1956.

Niebuhr, Reinhold. *The Children of Light and the Children of Darkness: The Vindication of Democracy and a Critique of its Traditional Defense.* New York: Charles Scribner's Sons, 1944.

Niebuhr, Reinhold. *The Irony of American History.* New York: Charles Scribner's Sons, 1952.

Niebuhr, Reinhold. *Moral Man and Immoral Society.* New York: Charles Scribner's Sons, 1932; reprint 1960.

Niebuhr, Reinhold. *The Nature and Destiny of Man, Volume I: Human Nature.* New York: Charles Scribner's Sons, 1941; reprint 1964.

Niebuhr, Reinhold. *The Nature and Destiny of Man, Volume II: Human Destiny.* New York: Charles Scribner's Sons, 1943; reprint 1964.

Nietzsche, Friedrich. *Beyond Good and Evil: Prelude to a Philosophy of the Future.* Trans. R. J. Hollingdale. New York: Penguin Books, 1990.

Nietzsche, Friedrich. *The Portable Nietzsche.* Trans. and ed. Walter Kaufmann. New York: Penguin Books, 1954.

Nietzsche, Friedrich. *Thus Spake Zarathustra: A Book for All and None.* Ed. Oscar Levy. New York: Russell & Russell, 1964.

Nolan, Hugh J., ed. *Pastoral Letters of the United States Catholic Bishops.* 4 vols. Washington, D.C.: United States Catholic Conference, 1984.

North, Gary. *The Sinai Strategy: Economics and the Ten Commandments.* Tyler, Tex.: Institute for Christian Economics, 1986.

North, Gary. *Unconditional Surrender: God's Program for Victory.* Tyler, Tex.: Institute for Christian Economics, 1981.

Novak, Michael. *Freedom with Justice: Catholic Social Thought and Liberal Institutions.* San Francisco: Harper & Row, 1984.

O'Brien, David J. *American Catholics and Social Reform: The New Deal Years.* New York: Oxford University Press, 1968.

Olasky, Marvin. *Renewing American Compassion.* New York: Free Press, 1996.

Oldfield, Duane Murray. *The Right and the Righteous: The Christian Right Confronts the Republican Party.* Westport, Conn.: Rowman & Littlefield, 1996.

Paris, Peter J. *The Social Teaching of the Black Churches.* Philadelphia: Fortress Press, 1985.

Pius XI. *On Reconstructing the Social Order (Quadragesimo Anno).* Trans. Francis Joseph Brown. Chicago: Outline Press, 1947.

Prebish, Charles S., and Kenneth K. Tanaka, eds. *The Faces of Buddhism in America.* Berkeley: University of California Press, 1998.

Presbyterian Church (U.S.A.). *Life Abundant: Values, Choices, and Health Care: The Responsibility and Role of the Presbyterian Church (U.S.A).* Louisville: Office of the General Assembly, 1988.

Presbyterian Church (U.S.A.). *Resolution on Christian Responsibility and a National Medical Plan.* Louisville: Office of the General Assembly, 1991.

Pyle, Ralph E. *Persistence and Change in the Protestant Establishment.* Westport, Conn.: Praeger, 1996.

Rajavaramuni, Phra. "Foundations of Buddhist Social Ethics." In *Ethics, Wealth and Salvation.* Eds. Russell F. Sizemore and Donald K. Swearer. Columbia: University of South Carolina Press, 1990, 29–53.

Rauschenbusch, Walter. *A Theology for the Social Gospel.* New York: Macmillan, 1917.

Rawlings, Charles W., and Janet Parker, eds. *Advocating Justice and Equity: Tools for Church Leaders.* Elkhart, Ind.: Economic Justice and Domestic Hunger Program Ministry of the National Council of Churches, 1998.

Reagan, Ronald. "Address to the Nation on the Economy." *Public Papers of the Presidents of the United States: Ronald Reagan, 1981.* Washington, D.C.: GPO, 1982.

Reagan, Ronald. "Inaugural Address: January 20, 1981." *Public Papers of the Presidents of the United States: Ronald Reagan, 1981.* Washington, D.C.: GPO, 1982.

Reagan, Ronald. "White House Report on the Program for Economic Recovery: February 18, 1981." *Public Papers of the Presidents of the United States: Ronald Reagan, 1981.* Washington, D.C.: GPO, 1982.

Reed, Ralph. *After the Revolution: How the Christian Coalition Is Impacting America.* Dallas: Word, 1996.

Reeves, Thomas C. *The Empty Church: The Suicide of Liberal Christianity.* New York: Free Press, 1996.

Reichley, A. James. *Religion in American Public Life.* Washington, D.C.: Brookings Institute, 1985.

Riemer, David Raphael. *The Prisoners of Welfare: Liberating America's Poor from Unemployment and Low Wages.* New York: Praeger, 1988.

Riemer, Neal. *The Future of the Democratic Revolution: Toward a More Prophetic Politics.* New York: Praeger, 1984.

Riemer, Neal. "Judaism: A Living Option for Modern Man." *Jewish Heritage* (fall 1961), 42–47.

Rogers, Kathryn. "S. Baptists Back Health Care Change." *St. Louis Post-Dispatch* (16 June 1994), 3C.

Roof, Wade Clark, and William McKinney. *American Mainline Religion: Its Changing Shape and Future.* New Brunswick: Rutgers University Press, 1987.

Rushdoony, Rousas John. *Politics of Guilt and Pity.* Fairfax: Thoburn Press, 1978.

Ryan, John A. *A Living Wage.* New York: Macmillan, 1906.

Saad, Lydia. "Public Has Cold Feet on Health Care Reform." *The Gallup Poll Monthly* (August 1994), 2.

Saperstein, David. "National Leaders Speak Out on Welfare Reform." Washington, D.C.: Religious Action Center of Reform Judaism (29 July 1996), URL: http//www.rj.org/rac/news/wlf2rds.html (accessed 3 October 1999), 1.

Schwarz, John E. *America's Hidden Success: A Reassessment of Twenty Years of Public Policy.* New York: W. W. Norton, 1983.

Seccombe, Karen. *So You Think I Drive a Cadillac? Welfare Recipients' Perspectives on the System and Its Reform.* Boston: Allyn & Bacon, 1999.

Shipps, Jan. "Morman Metamorphosis: The Neglected Story." *The Christian Century,* 113, 24 (14 August 1996), 784–87.

Shogren, Elizabeth. "Religious Groups Attack GOP Welfare, Medical Plans." *Los Angeles Times* (9 November 1995), A35.

Shogren, Elizabeth. "Senate, House on Own Paths in Welfare Debate." *Los Angeles Times* (16 September 1995), A4.

Shupe, Anson. "Militancy and Accommodation in the Third Civilization: The Case of Japan's Soka Gakkai Movement." In *Prophetic Religions and Politics*. Ed. Jeffery K Haddden and Anson Shupe. New York: Paragon House, 1986.

Sider, Ronald J. *Rich Christians in an Age of Hunger: A Biblical Study.* New York: Paulist Press, 1977.

Silk, Mark. "American Religion and Its Discontents." In *Religion and Cultural Change in American History.* URL: http//www.aar-site.org/scripts/AAR/public/silk.html. Harvard Divinity School, 1996.

Sizemore, Russell Foster. *Reinhold Niebuhr and the Rhetoric of Liberal Anti-Communism: Christian Realism and the Rise of the Cold War.* Ann Arbor: UMI, 1987.

Smith, Adam. *The Wealth of Nations.* New York: Modern Library, 1947; London, 1776.

Smith, Tom W. *Counting Flocks and Lost Sheep: Trends in Religious Preferences Since World War II.* Chicago: National Opinion Research Center, GSS Social Change Report No. 26, February 1988; Revised January 1991.

Smurl, James F. *The Burdens of Justice in Family, Education, Health Care, and Law.* Chicago: Loyola University Press, 1994.

Spencer, Herbert. *Social Statics.* New York: Robert Schalkenbach Foundation, 1970.

Springen, Donald K. *William Jennings Bryan: Orator of Small-Town America.* New York: Greenwood Press, 1991.

Sproul, R. C. *Money Matters: Making Sense of the Economic Issues That Affect You.* Wheaton, Ill.: Tyndale House Publishers, 1985.

Stark, Rodney, and William S. Bainbridge. *The Future of Religion.* Berkeley: University of California Press, 1985.

Steinfels, Peter. "Bishops Pass Resolution Warning against Abortion in Health Plan." *New York Times* (19 June 1993), 1, 47.

Strain, Charles R., ed. *Prophetic Visions and Economic Realities: Protestants, Jews and Catholics Confront the Bishops' Letter on the Economy.* Grand Rapids, Mich.: Eerdmans, 1989.

Sumner, William Graham. "The Forgotten Man." In *Social Darwinism: Selected Essays of William Graham Sumner.* Eds. William E. Leuchtenburg and Bernard Wishy. Englewood Cliffs: Prentice-Hall, 1963.

Tamari, Meir. *With All Your Possessions: Jewish Ethics and Economic Life.* New York: Free Press, 1987.

Tavris, Carol. *The Mismeasure of Woman.* New York: Simon & Schuster, 1992.

Thurman, Howard. *With Head and Heart: The Autobiography of Howard Thurman.* New York: Harcourt Brace Jovanovich, 1979.

Tocqueville, Alexis de. *Democracy in America.* Ed. J. P. Mayer; Trans. George Lawrence. New York: HarperPerennial, 1988; reprint, 1969.

Tucker, Robert C., ed. *The Marx-Engels Reader.* New York: W. W. Norton, 1978, 1972.

Turner, Douglas. "House Passes GOP Welfare-Overhaul Bill as Clinton Agrees to Sign It." *The Buffalo News* (1 August 1996), 1A.

Union of American Hebrew Congregations. "Health Care and Health Insurance."
    Washington D.C.: Religious Action Center of Reform Judaism, 1973.
Union of American Hebrew Congregations. "Reform of the Health Care System."
    Washington D.C.: Religious Action Center of Reform Judaism, 1993.
United Nations Development Programme. *Human Development Report 1998.* New
    York: Oxford University Press, 1998.
United Synagogue of Conservative Judaism. *Position Papers: Welfare Reform*
    (26 January 1995), URL: http//www.uscj.org/scripts/uscj/paper/Article.asp?
    ArticleID=24 (accessed 11 December 1998), 1.
Wald, Kenneth D. *Religion and Politics in the United States,* 3d ed. Washington,
    D.C.: CQ Press, 1997.
Wallis, Jim. *Who Is My Neighbor? Economics as if Values Matter: A Study Guide
    from the Editors of Sojourners.* Washington, D.C.: Sojourners, 1994.
Wallis, Jim. *Who Speaks for God? An Alternative to the New Christian Right: A
    New Politics of Compassion, Community, and Civility.* New York: Delacorte
    Press, 1996.
Walsh, Michael, and Brian Davies, eds. *Proclaiming Justice & Peace: Papal Docu-
    ments from Rerum Novarum* through *Centesimus Annus.* Mystic, Conn.:
    Twenty-Third Publications, Expanded, North American Edition, 1991.
Wangler, Thomas. E. "John Ireland's Emergence as a Liberal Catholic and Ameri-
    canist: 1875–1887." *Records of the American Catholic Historical Society*
    81 (1970).
Watson, Justin. *The Christian Coalition: Dreams of Restoration, Demands for
    Recognition.* New York: St. Martin's Press, 1997.
Wiesel, Elie. *The Night Trilogy.* New York: Noonday Press, 1988; reprint, 1972.
Williams, Oliver F., and John W. Houck, eds. *The Making of An Economic Vision:
    John Paul II's* On Social Concern. Lanham: University Press of America, 1991.
Winton, Ben. "Coalition Effort Worries Bishops: Pat Robertson Group Targets
    Catholics, Offers Politics at Odds with Church." *The Arizona Republic*
    (31 December 1995), A1.
Wuthnow, Robert. *God and Mammon in America.* New York: Free Press, 1994.
Zucchino, David. *Myth of the Welfare Queen.* New York: Scribner, 1997.

Index

ABOUT THE AUTHOR

ANDREW D. WALSH is Visiting Assistant Professor of Religious Studies at Indiana University-Purdue University at Indianapolis. Professor Walsh's earlier writings have focused on church-state issues. He has also written about how diverse religious communities in the United States sought to influence the public debates surrounding the Persian Gulf War.

ISBN 0-275-96611-9